MW00906798

── Food for ──
Christian Thought
Thirty-five Programs for Church Gatherings

BARBARA YOUNGER • LISA FLINN

Abingdon Press

FOOD FOR CHRISTIAN THOUGHT:
THIRTY-FIVE PROGRAMS FOR CHURCH GATHERINGS

Copyright © 1991 by Abingdon Press

All rights reserved.
No part of this work may be reproduced or transmitted in any
form or by any means, electronic or mechanical, including
photocopying and recording, or by any information storage or
retrieval system, except as may be expressly permitted by the
1976 Copyright Act or in writing from the publisher, except as
noted below. Requests for permission should be addressed in
writing to Abingdon Press, 201 Eighth Avenue South, Nashville,
TN 37203.

ISBN 0-687-13252-5

Scripture quotations, unless otherwise noted, are from the New
Revised Standard Version of the Bible, copyright © 1989 by the
Division of Christian Education of the National Council of
Churches of Christ in the U.S.A. Used by permission.

Permission is hereby granted to the purchaser to make copies for
program participants where specifically noted in text. See
asterisks.

MANUFACTURED IN THE UNITED STATES OF AMERICA

CONTENTS

INTRODUCTION

Crossing paths again and again in the church kitchen or Sunday school rooms and working on the same committees began our friendship and inspired this book. As we organized, baked, taught, hosted, and washed dishes, we observed that the most popular gatherings at our church featured food and that serving refreshments seemed to boost the attendance at classes and meetings. With this in mind, we wondered how we could creatively connect the always welcome food to Christian thoughts and themes. Turning to the Bible, we saw an opportunity to draw on the stories, songs, proverbs, laws, celebrations, parables, teachings, and miracles of the Scriptures. Using these references, we developed a variety of programs to enrich the spiritual significance of church gatherings. A few years ago we decided to turn our notes and recipes into this book so that we might share them with others.

Food for Christian Thought has six sections, each reflecting a different theme. All the programs are based on a passage of Scripture and feature a food or foods and an activity. A prayer, Bible verse, background information, food and material lists, and clear directions are organized into an easy-to-use format. The programs vary in length and style. An intergenerational resource, this book is designed to offer meaningful programs for almost any occasion from a committee meeting to a Bible study to a church supper.

The recipes used in the programs are collected into a separate section. Some of them are basic and are included for your convenience. Others, such as the recipe for flatbread, are more unusual. In some cases you may prefer to use a recipe of your own. Many of the programs do not even require cooking, and those that do often include shortcuts.

Although this book is addressed to the leader, the tasks involved in the program may be delegated. For clarity, the programs are quite structured. You may want to make some changes to meet the specific needs of your group. For instance, you may simplify the biblical background for young children or serve pancakes on Pancake Tuesday but forego the race. Let *Food for Christian Thought* spark your imagination. Create clever publicity, write a different prayer, add music, or make festive decorations to liven up the room. Don't forget a camera to take pictures for your church scrapbook. May God bless your gatherings!

Lisa Flinn
Barbara Younger
Hillsborough, North Carolina

I. TASTING THE GOODNESS OF THE WORD OF GOD

Salt: "You Are the Salt of the Earth"

Passing grains of salt to one another and speaking Jesus' words "You are the salt of the earth" move us to remember his challenge to those who follow him.

Matthew 5:13: "You are the salt of the earth; but if salt has lost its taste, how shall its saltiness be restored? It is no longer good for anything, but is thrown out and trodden under foot."

Preparations

Foods: salt

Materials: bowl(s)

At Home:
According to the expected size of the group, decide where you will hold the ceremony. A large group might gather in a sanctuary or fellowship hall. A small group can hold this ceremony anywhere from a classroom to a living room to a campfire circle.

Before the Gathering:
Pour salt into a bowl or bowls. One bowl is recommended for every twenty-five people. If the group is not to be seated in pews, the ceremony works nicely if chairs are arranged in a circle.

Gathering for the Passing of the Salt

After everyone is seated, begin by reading the following background information and explanation of the ceremony:

Today we honor the simplest of seasonings, salt. In ancient times the Hebrews were fortunate that the Dead Sea had nine times the concentration of mineral salt than any ocean, and salt supplies were abundant. Along with flavoring foods, salt was used to cure meat, pickle olives and vegetables, and keep fish from spoiling. Salt had medicinal uses too, and even newborn babies were rubbed with salt to ensure good health.

Since salt was such an essential of life in Bible times, it held spiritual significance for the Hebrews. Salt represented a perpetual covenant with God and was required in all food offerings as we learn from Leviticus 2:13: "You shall not let the salt of the covenant with your God be lacking from your cereal offerings; with all your offerings you shall offer salt."

In the New Testament the spiritual significance of salt continues through Jesus' words: "You are the salt of the earth" (Matthew 5:13) and "Have salt in yourselves and be at peace with one another" (Mark 9:50). With these words he creates a parallel between the purifying and preserving qualities of salt and the challenge of discipleship in this world. Later Paul writes in his epistle to the early Christians: "Let your speech always be gracious, seasoned with salt" (Colossians 4:6).

Today, almost two thousand years later, we will set salt apart from a common use to a spiritual one as we take part in a ceremony called "The Passing of the Salt." To affirm our perpetual covenant with God and our fellowship as Christians we will pass a bowl of salt to one another. When the bowl is passed to you take a pinch of salt, taste it, and offer the bowl to the person next to you, saying, "You are the salt of the earth."

Begin the ceremony by offering the bowl to someone in the group. With a large group start bowls at several locations. When everyone has tasted the salt, accept the bowl from the last person and taste the salt yourself. Close with the following benediction:

Let your speech always be gracious, seasoned with salt, so that you may know how you ought to answer everyone. Have salt in yourselves and be at peace with one another. Amen.

Honey: "Pleasant Words Are Like Honeycomb"

Just a taste of honey and a kind word remind us of an age-old proverb.

Proverbs 16:24: "Pleasant words are like a honeycomb, sweetness to the soul and health to the body."

Preparations

Foods: honey

Materials: bowl; spoon or dipper; toothpicks, straws, or wooden spoons

Before the Gathering:
Place the honey, and the honeycomb if available, in a bowl. Toothpicks, straws, or wooden spoons can be put in another bowl or basket.

Gathering to Taste Honey

After the group is seated, hold up the bowl of honey. Spoon some honey and allow it to drip back into the bowl. Next, read or tell the biblical background:

We know that bees must have been busy in biblical times because honey is mentioned throughout the Bible from Genesis (Gen. 43:11) to Revelation (Rev. 10:9). Honey was cultivated as well as recovered in the wilderness from trees and rocks. Artificial honey was made from dates, figs, and grapes.

The sweet tooth seems to have existed then just as it does today, and honey, the most prevalent of sweeteners, was thought of with great fondness. Honey is listed in Genesis 43:11 as one of the "choice fruits of the

7

land," and the Promised Land is described over and over again as a "land flowing with milk and honey" (Exodus 3:8). Proverbs 16:24 makes a lovely analogy between kind speech and honey: (Read Proverbs 16:24).

Tell the group that to help them remember this important thought, they will now taste some honey and exchange kind words.

Pass the bowl of honey and tasting utensils to each participant. When everyone has had a taste, explain the Kind Word Chain:

The first person begins by saying a kind word to the person on his or her right. That person then says a kind word to the person on his or her right. This continues until the chain is complete.

Close the honey tasting with the following prayer:
Dear God,
The next time we are about to utter an unkind word, stop us. Remind us of this taste of honey. Amen.

Grapes: "Abide in Me and I in You"

After hearing the lesson of the vinedresser, weave a wreath as a keepsake.

John 15:5: "I am the vine, you are the branches. Those who abide in me and I in them bear much fruit."

Preparations

Foods: seedless grapes

Materials: locally growing vines, such as honeysuckle or grape, cut in lengths of two to three feet; ribbon, ¼ to ½ inch width, 14 inches in length, one per wreath; napkins

At Home:
Rinse grapes and separate the bunches into small clusters.
After you locate vines, cut them into 2-foot to 3-foot lengths. Whether your vine branches are locally cut or purchased, you may find them easier to transport and distribute if they are rolled individually in a sheet of newspaper.
Choose ribbon and pre-cut into 14-inch lengths.

Before the Gathering:
Place grape clusters on napkins and arrange on a platter. Place the platter on the meeting table. Lay the vines and ribbon close by.

Gathering to Weave Branches

Begin with a prayer:
Heavenly Father,
As we eat the fruit of the vine and hold the pruned branches in our hands, we remember Jesus' life-giving connection to us. Amen.

Invite all to nibble on the grapes as you present the Bible background:

From ancient days to present ones, grapes have been a main agricultural crop of the Holy Land. The rocky hill-country provided a perfect setting for the abundant, large grapes described in Numbers 13:23. Sojourners returned with "a branch with a single cluster of grapes, and they carried it on a pole between two of them."

In early times, vineyards were prepared by clearing away the many stones and forming them into walls to hold the soil and rainfall. The vines were planted in rows and allowed, when young, to run along the ground. The law of Moses prevented any harvest of the fruit until the vine was three years old. Eventually vines were trained to grow on the stone walls, on frames, or over trees. The vinedresser trimmed damaged branches in March. When grape clusters formed, any barren branches were pruned. Once again, when new fruit appeared, the nonproductive branches were trimmed away. In the fall grapes were ready to harvest. Wine, raisins, vinegar, juice, and debash, which was similar to jelly, were products of the harvest.

The tending of the vineyard is compared to our productivity as Christians in John 15. Listen to the words of Jesus: (Read John 15:1-9).

We are grateful for the writings of John, which help us better understand our relationship to God and to each other.

Now that we have enjoyed the fruit of a good branch, let us remember the lesson of the barren branch by weaving a small wreath.

Give each person a length of vine and explain how to weave the wreath:

Rest the branch horizontally in your hands. Move your hands toward each other, allowing the branch to slide across your palms until your hands are about nine inches apart, with equal lengths of vine hanging loose on either end. Use the thumb and fingertips of each hand to grasp the vine, and make a circle by moving thumbs toward each other. The branch ends will cross. Use one forefinger and thumb to grasp both stems where they cross. This frees the other hand to grasp one side of the crossed branches and begin to wrap it as it is inclined. After one branch has been wrapped several times, the circle will hold together naturally and the wrapping continues more easily. When one end is completely wrapped, wrap the other end as it is inclined. To finish, tie a bow on the wreath.

When the wreaths are finished, tell the wreath-makers to hang them in their homes as a souvenir of the lesson of the vinedresser.

Vinegar: "I Thirst"

Hearing Jesus' humble request from the cross, "I thirst," and touching vinegar to our own lips deepens our understanding of his sacrifice.

John 19:28: "After this, when Jesus knew that all was finished, he said (in order to fulfill the scripture), 'I am thirsty.' "

Preparations

Foods: wine vinegar; hyssop or lettuce

Materials: bowls; napkins

At Home:
Wash hyssop or lettuce. Tear the leaves into small pieces, drain, and arrange in a bowl.

Before the Gathering:
Pour vinegar into a small bowl. If a larger group is expected, you may want to use several bowls. Set the vinegar on a table along with the hyssop or lettuce and napkins.

Gathering to Taste Vinegar

Begin the tasting by reading John's account of the moments before Jesus' death (John 19:28-30). After the reading, relate the following background:

Vinegar was commonly available in biblical times since it is made from wine. Where water supplies were limited, it was mixed with oil to provide a drink. Roman soldiers drank a type of sour wine called *acetum,* which translates "vinegar." Most likely this is what was offered to the dying Jesus.

In John's account, the vinegar is given to Jesus on a leaf of hyssop, a shrubby herb plentiful in biblical times. In fact, the Passover blood was applied to the doorposts with a bunch of hyssop (Exodus 2:22). Noted for its refreshing flavor, similar to mint, hyssop was thought to have purifying powers as Psalm 51:7 suggests: "Purge me with hyssop, and I shall be clean."

Some biblical scholars believe that giving vinegar to Jesus was not a gesture of compassion but one of mockery. John writes that Jesus spoke the words "I am thirsty" to fulfill the Scripture. This Scripture may be Psalm 69:21:
They gave me poison for food,
and for my thirst they gave me vinegar to drink.
For whatever reason vinegar was given to Jesus, a taste of vinegar, pungent to most palates, will remind us of the cruelty of his death on the cross.

If you were fortunate enough to locate hyssop, be sure to let the group know this. If using lettuce, mention that it is serving as a substitute for hyssop.

To make this occasion meditative, ask that the tasting be done in silence. Pass the bowls around the table. Each person is to dip the hyssop or lettuce into the vinegar. When everyone has tasted, conclude with a prayer:

Heavenly Father,
With this taste of vinegar, fill our hearts with a deeper understanding of the suffering Jesus endured for our salvation. In his name we pray. Amen.

Water: "Even a Cup of Cold Water"

A drink of water from a paper cup becomes a caring gesture in this lighthearted relay game.

Matthew 10:42: "And whoever gives even a cup of cold water to one of these little ones in the name of a disciple—truly I tell you, none of these will lose their reward."

Preparations

Foods: water

Materials: two unbreakable pitchers; small paper cups; two lengths of masking tape or yarn.

Before the Gathering
The Cup of Cold Water Relay works best outdoors or in a large room such as a fellowship hall. On each end of a table, place the pitchers filled with water. Next to each pitcher place a stack of paper cups. Use two lengths of yarn or tape, placed at least twenty feet from the table, to serve as markers.

Gathering to Taste Water

After you welcome the group, offer the following biblical background:

In a few minutes we will play a game called The Cup of Cold Water Relay. The water for this game was taken from a nearby faucet. In biblical times it wasn't as easy to fill a pitcher with water as it is today. Water supplies depended mainly on rainfall, which was scarce in the summer. This lack of water caused springs to dry up.
Cisterns were used to collect rain water or were filled by conduits connected to a spring. Wells were often dug at the location of an underground spring. Women carried water in jugs from these wells, which were usually located at the gate to the city. It was at a well that Jesus promised the woman of Samaria "those who drink of the water that I will give them will never be thirsty" (John 4:14).
For the thirsty, water was an available drink. A gracious host or hostess offered a cup of water to any visitor, friend or stranger. Jesus refers to this custom when he talks to his disciples about their mission: (Read Matthew 10:42).

With a smile, tell the group that they will now participate in a challenging athletic event, The Cup of Cold Water Relay. Divide the group into two teams. Send one member of each team to the markers. The rest of the team should line up behind a set of pitchers and cups on the table.
Explain the relay:

The first person in line is to fill a cup with water and rush it to the team member at the markers. That person must drink the water and hurry back to

11

the end of the line. The team member who carried water now stands at the marker. The next person in line brings water to that team member. The relay continues until an entire team has both carried water and drunk it.

After congratulating the winners, ask the entire group to join hands in a circle. Conclude with a prayer:

Dear God,
Send us into the world to be disciples of the good news of the living water of Jesus Christ. In his name we pray. Amen.

Bread: "Life to the World"

A loaf of fresh bread passed around a table is a great way to begin any meeting.

John 6:33 "For the bread of God is that which comes down from heaven and gives life to the world."

Preparations

Foods: Bowl Bread (Recipe Collection) or bakery bread; beverages

Materials: serving basket; cloth napkin or tea towel; napkins; cups

At Home:
Bake Bowl Bread or purchase freshly baked bread. Wrap the bread in a cloth and place it in a basket.

Before the Gathering:
Place the basket of bread on the meeting table.
Prepare desired beverages and put out cups and napkins.

Gathering for the Breaking of Bread

While people are arriving loosen the cloth and let the sight of fresh bread welcome them to the table.
Begin by asking everyone to share a thought about bread—nostalgic, practical, spiritual, or comic. When your turn comes, relate the following biblical information:

The baking of bread was a daily task in biblical times. Wheat and barley flour were mixed into a dough and kneaded in a wooden bowl. When ready, the dough was patted into a flat circle and pricked. Finally, it was usually placed over a bowl or jar to bake.
Leavened bread was most commonly used, except during the seven days of Passover or when presented as an offering.

Jesus uses familiar aspects of everyday life to illustrate his teachings. He tells of the leavening of bread to describe the power of heaven (Matthew 13:35). In teaching his disciples how to pray he incorporates "daily bread" into the prayer (Matthew 6:11). At the Last Supper, Jesus asks his disciples to remember him whenever they break bread. Since that time, Christians have partaken of bread in Holy Communion with Jesus Christ.

In the Gospel of John, Jesus calls himself "the bread of life" as he addresses a crowd: (Read John 6:28-35).

Then, invite the group to pray together before breaking bread:

Holy Father,
We thank you for the freshly baked bread that sustains our bodies and for the miracle bread that nourishes our souls. Your Son, the Bread of Life, taught us to pray, saying: *(all repeat The Lord's Prayer)*

Pass the basket around the table, asking each person to break off a bit of bread. Send the loaf around again if there is any left.

II. SHARING STORIES OF THE OLD AND NEW COVENANTS

The Creation: Day and Night Cookies

Frost an old-fashioned Day and Night Cookie and think about the magnificence of God's creation.

Genesis 1:5: "God called the light Day and the darkness he called Night. And there was evening and there was morning, one day."

Preparations

Foods: Day and Night Cookies (Recipe Collection) or purchase large sugar cookies; Butter Frosting (Recipe Collection) or two 16-ounce cans of prepared frosting; beverages

Materials: plates; napkins; cups; knives

At Home:
This activity works well in a Sunday school class or as a vacation church school activity. Adults will enjoy this delicious treat too, perhaps at the conclusion of a Bible study or meeting.
Bake Day and Night Cookies. If you choose not to bake, purchase large sugar cookies.
Mix Butter Frosting and put it into bowls suitable for transporting to the gathering. If you wish, purchase chocolate and vanilla prepared frosting.

Before the Gathering:
Place the cookies on a platter. Uncover homemade frosting or open canned frosting. Set out plates, cups, napkins, and knives. Prepare beverages.

Gather to Frost Day and Night Cookies

Tell the group that you are going to read them the story of the creation. Read Genesis 1.
After the reading, ask everyone to close his or her eyes and picture God's creation as you pray a prayer of thanksgiving. Say the prayer slowly, allowing time for the listeners to visualize each line:

Heavenly Father,
    Hear our prayer of thanksgiving for the wonders of your creation:
    We thank you
    For day and night,
    For spring and fall, summer and winter,
    For heaven and earth and sea,
    For trees and plants and flowers,

For the sun and the moon and the stars,
For living creatures of sea and earth and air,
For human beings created in your image, male and female,
For the magnificence of your world
We pray this prayer of thanksgiving. Amen.

After the prayer announce that you will now celebrate one part of the creation story, the creation of day and night.

Demonstrate how to turn an ordinary cookie into a Day and Night Cookie. Frost one half with vanilla frosting (day) and the other half with chocolate frosting (night).

Give each person a cookie, a plate, a knife, and a napkin. Let the frosting begin!

After the cookies are frosted, serve the beverages. Indulge.

Noah's Ark: "My Bow in the Cloud"

Animal Crackers and Rainbow Cake would have been a welcome treat on the ark.

Genesis 9:13: "I set my bow in the clouds, and it shall be a sign of the covenant between me and the earth."

Preparations

Foods: Animal Crackers; Rainbow Cake (Recipe Collection); Flood Punch (Recipe Collection)

Materials: Critter Collage: posterboard, computer paper; or shelf paper; old magazines; scissors; glue
story: a toy Noah's ark, picture book, or flannel board story
cups; napkins; punch bowl and ladle; plates
favors (optional): pencils, stickers, or bookmarks

At Home:
This activity works well with a group of children or as a family event.

Purchase Animal Crackers and the ingredients for Flood Punch and Rainbow Cake. Bake the cake.

Collect materials for the Critter Collage. Magazines with lots of photographs of animals such as *National Geographic* or *Ranger Rick* will be especially useful. If you can't find enough pictures of animals, the collage can be made of construction paper animals or animals drawn with crayon or marker.

Prepare to tell the story of Noah using a toy Noah's ark, a picture book such as Peter Spier's *Noah's Ark,* or a flannel board set.

Rainbow stickers, pencils, or bookmarks make nice take-home favors.

15

Before the Gathering:

Set out craft supplies on tables. Be sure to unroll any shelf paper so it will flatten.

Using a serrated knife, slice the cake. Place the cake and the Animal Crackers on plates. Mix the punch. Keep the refreshments a surprise.

Gathering for the Story of Noah's Ark

After everyone is seated, present the story of Noah's ark. Here are some questions to ask when the story is finished:

Do you think that Noah was afraid when God asked him to build the ark? Would you rather have been in charge of the lions, the snakes, the pelicans, or the turtles? What do you suppose Noah and his family thought about during those long days on the ark? What is the promise that God made with the rainbow?

After the discussion, invite the group to make a collage of the many animals that sailed on the ark.

When the Critter Collage is finished, hold it up for all to admire. Let the artists know that it will be hung for all who visit the church to see. Ask everyone to help you clean up. Wash sticky hands if necessary.

Put the punch bowl on a table along with the Rainbow Cake and Animal Crackers.

Call everyone to gather around the table. Explain that the Flood Punch represents the waters of the flood, and the cake honors God's rainbow promise, and the Animal Crackers are to remember the animals on the ark.

Ask everyone to join hands around the table. Then pray:

Dear God,
    We thank you for Noah and his family, the sturdy ark, the animals, the dove and her olive branch, and your promise of the rainbow. Amen.

Serve the refreshments. Before the group begins to leave give out favors, if you have brought them.

Be certain that the collage is hung for all to admire in the weeks to come.

Feeding of the Five Thousand: A Luncheon of Loaves and Fishes

Baskets, fish banners, and loaves of barley bread create a festive mood for feeding a crowd!

John 6:9: "There is a boy here who has five barley loaves and two fish. But what are they among so many?"

Preparations

Foods: Barley Bread (Recipe Collection) or bakery loaves; butter or margarine; potluck dishes with a fish theme; beverages

Materials: baskets; banners and garlands (shelf or craft paper, crayons, markers, paint, yarn or ribbon, tape); sponges or stencils; plates; napkins; cups; forks; knives; spoons

At Home:

This luncheon idea is quite flexible in the areas of menu and activity. Use your imagination as you shape this event to fit your expected group.

A children's Sunday school class will enjoy plates of tuna fish sandwiches and a mural painting project. The Couples Club might select a menu of smoked fish, good cheeses, and opt for no art activity. A suggestion for the general congregation could be a "favorite fish or seafood dish" potluck supper with paper tablecloths for all to decorate. Essential to all options, however, are the loaves of bread that remind us of the miracle of the loaves and fishes.

Prepare bread according to the Barley Bread recipe or purchase loaves from a bakery.

Round up as many baskets as possible for centerpieces and also suggest that potluck dishes be brought in baskets.

Call on the artists of the congregation to fashion paper fish banners and garlands for decorations. These can be designed with crayons, markers, sponge paints, or stencils. Tape or hang large fish on the walls and string smaller fish together to make garlands.

Goldfish crackers are popular with all ages and make a delicious favor tied in a square of netting or nestled in a tiny basket.

Before the Gathering:

Decorate with banners, garlands, and baskets.

Prepare serving tables, dining tables, place settings, and beverages. The baskets of bread should be put on the dining tables, along with butter or margarine.

If an art activity is planned, get the supplies ready. The art activity can be done either as the group is arriving or after the meal.

Gathering for a Luncheon of Loaves and Fishes

Ask everyone assembled to be seated to listen to a story of wonders and miracles.

Read John 6:1-21.

Next, lead the group in prayer, asking them to respond "Thanks be to God" after each statement you make.

LEADER: God of miracles, we give thanks for the signs and wonders revealed to humankind to strengthen our belief.

ALL: **Thanks be to God.**

LEADER:	We are grateful that these miracles have relieved human need and suffering.
ALL:	**Thanks be to God.**
LEADER:	We are thankful for your Messenger and our Messiah, Jesus Christ, who recognizes our hunger, in both body and spirit.
ALL:	**Thanks be to God.**
LEADER:	Amen.

Let the luncheon begin!

Jesus Visits Martha and Mary: A Skit for Three Players

We are reminded that "man cannot live by bread alone" by watching a skit about Martha, Mary, and Jesus.

Luke 10:38: "Now as they went on their way, he entered a certain village, where a woman named Martha welcomed him into her home."

Preparations

Materials: an apron; small table; chair or bench; jug or pitcher; bowls; plates; and wooden spoons

At Home:
The skit retells the story of Jesus' visit to Martha and Mary. It makes a thought-provoking introduction to a church meal or as an opening to a meeting or Bible study.

Recruit three players to be Martha, Mary, and Jesus. Give them photocopies* of the skit. Although they need not memorize their lines, they should rehearse before presenting the skit to the group.

Decide where you will stage the skit. One end of a fellowship hall or a larger meeting room will be fine since not much space is required.

Gather props. You will need a small table where Martha will work and a chair or bench for Jesus. Martha is to wear an apron. Mary enters carrying a jug, and Martha uses bowls, spoons, and plates to prepare the meal. Although contemporary kitchenware will do, pottery or stoneware and wooden spoons have a more biblical look.

Before the Gathering:
Set the stage for the skit. Martha's table, with her kitchenware on it, should be in the foreground. Jesus' chair or bench should be behind and to the right or left of the table.

Chairs for the audience can be set to face the stage. If the group is to be seated at tables, chairs should be turned to face the stage.

18

Lenten Thoughts

Throughout Lent, we will be offering Devotions for Lent.

Dietrich Bonhoeffer (1906- 1945) ranks high on any list of Christian Leaders of the twentieth century. He was a clear-headed thinker and a plain spoken German Lutheran minister. He was personally committed to Christ in such a way that led him to face imprisonment and death at the hands of the Nazis

These may seem like lofty heights on which to focus but it does give us something to work toward and place to journey. A guide for Lent at the turn of a troubled century!

DAILY WE MUST 'PUSH THROUGH UNBELIEF TO REACH FAITH AND WREST IT FROM GOD'

Ask in faith, never doubting, for the one who doubts is like a wave of the sea, driven and tossed by the wind. James 1:6

You do not have your belief once and for all. Your belief demands to be won anew tomorrow and the day after tomorrow; indeed, it demands to be won anew with every new day. God gives us always just precisely so much faith as we need for the present day. Faith is the daily bread which God gives us. You know the manna story: while the children of Israel were in the wilderness, they received it every day, but as soon as they tried to store it up for the next day, it spoiled. So it is with God's gifts. So it is with faith too. Either we receive it anew every day or it decays. One day is long enough to keep faith.

Every morning brings a new struggle to push through all the unbelief, through all the littleness of faith, through all the vagueness and confusion, through all the faintheartedness and uncertainty, to reach faith and wrest it from God.

Do I appreciate the importance of daily devotion? Do I realize the great need that my faith grow daily lest I begin to slip backwards?

Gathering for a Skit

Invite the group to be seated. Say the following:

In just a few moments we will see a skit with three players: Martha and Mary, two sisters from Bethany, and Jesus.

The Gospel tells us that Jesus loved Martha and Mary and their brother, Lazarus, whom Jesus raises from the dead (John 11:1-45). Mary appears to be the more intent believer in the story our skit is based upon. Yet Martha, who confesses her faith in Jesus before the raising of Lazarus (John 11:27), shows her love and respect for Jesus by her desire to be a good hostess and make him comfortable in her home. Let's watch and see what Jesus tells her:

Jesus Visits Martha and Mary

(Martha is working at a table when there is a knock on the door.)

MARTHA: Teacher. How good to have you visit my home.

JESUS: Hello, Martha. I'm happy to see you. Where is Mary?

MARTHA: She went to the well to get water.

(Mary enters carrying a jug of water)

MARY: Jesus! I'm so glad that you are here.

JESUS: Hello, Mary.

MARTHA: Please sit down, Jesus. I will have the meal ready in just a little while.

(Martha returns to her table to continue preparing the meal. Mary walks Jesus to his seat. He sits down and she sits at his feet. Jesus silently mimics conversation as Mary intently listens. She responds occasionally, perhaps asking questions. Meanwhile, Martha works frantically. She uses her plates, spoons, and bowls to mix, stir, and serve imaginary food. Martha begins to turn her head and eye Mary, noticeably annoyed that she isn't helping. In a few moments she stops what she is doing and walks over to Jesus.)

MARTHA: *(Hands on hips)* Jesus, don't you care that my sister isn't helping me? She has left me to do all the work and serve alone.

JESUS: *(Slowly)* Martha, Martha. You are anxious and troubled about so many things. Mary has chosen the right thing, and it will not be taken away from her.

(Martha slowly unties her apron and takes it off. She sits down with Jesus and Mary. He touches her on the shoulder and smiles.)

After the skit, thank the players. Then offer a prayer:

19

Lord God,

Jesus' words to Martha speak to Christians today. Our church keeps us so busy: Sunday school classes, potluck suppers, choir rehearsals, building funds, Christmas pageants, and much, much more. Let us not forget the right thing, the message of Jesus Christ to the world.

We pray in his name. Amen.

The Resurrection: "Come and Have Breakfast"

Have breakfast together and imagine the disciples' amazement and joy at their early morning meeting with Jesus.

John 21:12: "Jesus said to them 'Come and have breakfast.' Now none of the disciples dared to ask him 'Who are you?' because they knew it was the Lord."

Preparations

Foods: potluck breakfast dishes; beverages

Materials: invitations; photocopies of prayer; plates; napkins; cups; knives; forks; spoons

At Home:

Jesus' invitation to the disciples to have breakfast was of special significance. Make your breakfast special by extending personal invitations. If the group is to be small or medium in size, you may want to send written invitations. For a larger group or the general congregation, you may prefer to use a poster, bulletin insert, or newsletter. Whatever type of invitation you choose, please echo Jesus' simple yet perfect words "Come and have breakfast." As well as telling date, time, and location, be sure to indicate that it is to be a potluck breakfast.

Since Jesus was cooking breakfast over a charcoal fire, you may want to consider an outdoor setting.

Find a person who enjoys reading aloud to share John 20–21:14 with the breakfasters.

Make photocopies* of the prayer for the group to read.

Before the Gathering:

Set up a serving table and dining tables. Arrange cups, plates, napkins, serving utensils, knives, forks, and spoons.

Prepare beverages.

Place a copy of the prayer at each place or on each seat.

Gathering to Have Breakfast

Direct people to place potluck dishes on the serving table and encourage everyone to be seated.

When you are ready, introduce the reader. Explain that he or she will read John's story of Jesus' Resurrection appearances to Mary Magdalene and to the disciples.

Follow the reading by leading the group in the prayer:

LEADER: Lord, hear our prayer this morning.

ALL: **Lord, we give you thanks that when Mary sought you in the tomb, instead she found you transformed by new life.**

LEADER: "Go to my brethren and tell them I am ascending to my Father and your Father, my God and your God."

ALL: **We are grateful that the fearful disciples hidden behind locked doors could see you and witness the miracle of resurrection.**

LEADER: "Peace be with you."

ALL: **We give thanks for the skepticism of Thomas, whose example makes clear to us our need for faith.**

LEADER: "Blessed are those who have not seen yet believe."

ALL: **We are grateful that you so often illustrate the spiritual significance of breaking bread together.**

LEADER: "Come and have breakfast."

To start the breakfast, invite anyone named Mary, Simon, Thomas, Nathaniel, or Peter to be the first in line.

III. KEEPING HOLY DAYS AND HOLIDAYS

"O Come, O Come, Emmanuel": Stir-up Sunday Cake

Years ago this holiday cake was the first to be baked before Christmas.

Isaiah 40:5: "Then the glory of the LORD shall be revealed, and all people shall see it together, for the mouth of the LORD has spoken."

Preparations

Foods: Stir-up Sunday Cake (Recipe Collection) or purchased fruitcake; beverages

Materials: hymnals; plates; cups; napkins; forks

At Home
   Stir-up Sunday is the Sunday before the first Sunday of Advent. However, you may wish to serve Stir-up Sunday Cake at any Advent gathering.
   Bake the Stir-up Sunday Cake or purchase a fruitcake. Recruit someone to play the piano or another instrument if you wish to have accompaniment to the singing of the carol.

Before the Gathering:
   Cut the cake and arrange the slices on a plate.
   Prepare beverages and set out plates, cups, napkins, and forks.

Gathering for Stir-up Sunday Cake

After everyone is seated, pass out hymnals for singing "O Come, O Come, Emmanuel." After the carol has been sung, read Isaiah 40:3-5.
   Following the reading, give a brief history of Advent:

The exact day of Jesus' birth is not known, but by the fifth century, the date of December 25 was set. As the custom of celebrating Christmas grew, a time of spiritual preparation for this holy day was thought to be appropriate. This period of time before Christmas was named "Advent," which means "coming." Originally Advent began in mid-November but by the ninth century the fourth Sunday before Christmas Day marked its beginning.
   At one time Advent was kept as a time of solemn preparation, much like Lent. As Christmas traditions grew, Advent became a joyous time of anticipation and festivity, as it is today.

Ask the group to think about Advent traditions such as the Advent wreath, decorating the tree, and holiday baking. Ask each person to name a favorite Advent activity and tell why it is special.
   After the discussion, announce to the group that they are soon to be served Stir-up Sunday Cake, which in days gone by was the first holiday treat to be baked. Give the background behind this cake:

Stir-up Sunday Cake takes its name from Stir-up Sunday, the Sunday before the first Sunday in Advent. Stir-up Sunday was inspired by the opening words for the collect of the day: "Stir up we beseech thee, O Lord, the wills of thy faithful people." According to some accounts the cake was served on this Sunday. Others say that the cake was baked on this day and allowed to age until Christmas. All members of the household would take a turn stirring the batter. Each person was to make a wish while stirring the batter.

A collect is a short prayer said during a worship service before a reading from the Bible. The collect varies from day to day. Before the cake is served, pray the collect for Stir-up Sunday:

Stir up, we beseech thee, O Lord, the wills of thy faithful people; that they, plenteously bringing forth the fruit of good works, may of thee be plenteously rewarded; through Jesus Christ our Lord. Amen.

Serve the cake and enjoy Advent conversation. (No complaining about too much to do and too little time.)

Christmas Caroling: A New Refreshment for an Old Custom

Reward carolers with steaming mugs of white chocolate.

Luke 2:13-14: "And suddenly there was with the angel a multitude of the heavenly host, praising God and saying,
'Glory to God in the highest heaven,
and on earth peace among those whom he favors.' "

Preparations

Foods: White Christmas Hot Chocolate (Recipe Collection); plates of Christmas treats

Materials: sheet music, hymnals, or songbooks; angel table decorations; holiday tablecloth; plates; mugs or insulated cups; napkins

At Home:
This holiday party is a warm way to greet returning carolers or a nice conclusion to a caroling service.
Consider what Christmas angel decorations you or a friend might have to dress up the serving table.
If you are organizing the carolers, determine what music and accompaniment are needed.
Look over the recipe for White Christmas Hot Chocolate to see what ingredients you need and how much you wish to prepare at home. Your carolers may also enjoy hot tea, coffee, or cider.
Ask your committee or the participants to bring plates of holiday treats.

Before the Gathering:

Arrange and decorate the serving tables. Set out plates, mugs, napkins, and treats.

Heat the beverages. Some steps may be taken to keep the beverages warm until the caroling is finished by using thermal carafes or crockpots.

Gathering to Sing Christmas Carols

Welcome all heralders with a reading from Luke 2:8-14.

Follow the good news from the Bible with a history of caroling:

We enjoy participating in holiday traditions, although we sometimes do not know their origins.

Caroling and the word *carol* have their earliest roots in Greece. In ancient days the Greeks performed a circle dance called "choralein" to flute music. Over time, the Romans absorbed the custom and during their conquests introduced the circle dance to the Britons. In the Middle Ages, the English substituted singing voices for flute playing, and the dance became known as a "carol." Eventually the circle dance was left off, and the singing alone was called "caroling."

Christian hymns, written in Latin verse, were spread throughout Europe by troubadours. By the fifteenth century the hymns were translated and sung in English.

Later, when Cromwell ruled Britain during the mid-1600s, caroling and Christmas festivities were banned. Any type of joyful celebration was carried on secretly. However, the tradition survived, in part because it was practiced in other countries. In Austria, Father Mohr and organist Franz Gruber composed "Silent Night," which was sung to guitar accompaniment, since the organ was broken. In the American colonies, people ranging from the Huron Indians to the Moravian immigrants sang Christmas carols with joy.

Now tell the group that they will carry on this beloved tradition when they lift their voices in song. Before the caroling begins, offer a prayer:

God of Yesterday and Today,
We will sing our thanks and praise as we retell the coming of Jesus through carols. We will rejoice by lifting our hearts and voices to proclaim to the modern world the ancient tidings of Christ's birth. Amen.

When the caroling is finished, surprise the group with White Christmas Hot Chocolate!

St. Valentine's Day: "A New Commandment I Give to You"

Craft Christian valentines with messages from the heart.

John 13:34-35: "A new commandment I give to you, that you love one another; even as I have loved you, that you also love one another. By this all men will know that you are my disciples, if you love one another."

Preparations

Foods: Valentine Pizza (Recipe Collection); Bible Garden Salad (Recipe Collection); Scripture Salad Dressing (Recipe Collection); beverages

Materials: Pizza: cookie sheets; paring knife; bowls; plates; cups; napkins; forks; and spoons
Valentines: colored paper; paper lace doilies; fabric and craft trimmings; markers; crayons; glue; scissors
Also helpful: stencils; stickers; rubber stamps and pads; calligraphy pens; old greeting cards

At Home:
Consult the Recipe Collection for the pizza, salad, and dressing ingredients and directions.
Collect supplies for the handmade valentines. You may wish to find books about St. Valentine's Day at your library for craft suggestions.
Consider to whom the valentines might be sent.
Using sheets of construction paper, cut out large hearts and on them print "heart" Bible verses. These will be used in the prayer and in card making. The verses are: Matthew 5:8; I Samuel 16:7; I Peter 1:22; Hebrews 10:22; Matthew 6:21; Matthew 22:37; John 14:27; Psalm 28:7; and Colossians 3:15.

Before the Gathering:
Prepare the pizzas for baking.
Set out the ingredients that the group will use to garnish their own pizzas. Keep the salad chilled. Have the plates, cups, napkins, and forks handy. Prepare beverages.
On the craft tables, display all of the decorating items and any idea books you have found.

Gathering to Craft Valentines

Direct everyone to the craft tables. Open the gathering with the words of Jesus in John 13:34-35.
After the reading, share the history of St. Valentine's Day:

St. Valentine's Day probably dates back to pagan times in Italy. When Rome was only a shepherds' village, a spring festival was created to honor the god of animal herds and the land. The ancient celebration, known as Lupercalia, was also associated with the founders of Rome, Romulus and Remus, orphaned babies kept alive by a wolf. The Latin word for wolf is *lupus*.
The calendar month named *February* may stem from the ritual reenactment of the story of Romulus and Remus. Two young boys raced from a cave through the village streets waving leather thongs. If any young

25

woman was touched by the thongs, this was an omen of good luck for her in childbearing. The Latin word *februs* was the name of the special thong, and its root meaning was "to purify."

In the days of the Roman Empire the festival of Lupercalia was set on February 14. The festival had come to involve the drawing of names to pair young men and young women. When the Romans conquered foreign lands, they carried with them the Lupercalia as well as other customs.

An Italian priest named Valentine, who lived in the third century A.D., is honored by the renaming of the Lupercalia. Evidently, Valentine was known for his kind words, good deeds, and possibly a miracle. However, he was in disfavor with someone in the government and was made a martyr by beheading on February 14. This probably took place at the festival. History tells us of the general practice of such gory entertainment in those times.

While Rome was still a great empire, the conversion to Christianity occurred. The formerly pagan customs, which had been widely spread throughout Europe and the Mediterranean, were transformed into Christian holidays. February 14 became St. Valentine's Day.

Habits and customs are hard to change, and in England the drawing of names to pair couples persisted on February 14. Later the day became a time for declarations of love, proposals, and the exchanging of letters, tokens, and gifts.

By the 1800s printing machines produced a ready-made valentine card, which sparked the interest of the English and Americans. In the last century, St. Valentine's Day has become, more than anything else, a day for exchanging cards between friends and loved ones.

After the history, pass out the large paper hearts with the Bible verses printed on them to some members of the group. Tell them that the hearts are to be read as part of the prayer. You will begin, then motion to the person on your left, and those holding hearts will read successively. You will end the prayer.

> Loving God,
> We extol these words of Scripture for they are a blessing and a comfort to us:
> (The hearts are read.)
> And we conclude with the excellent explanation of our mission in the words of Paul: "You yourselves are our letter, written on our hearts, to be known and read by all; and you show that you are a letter from Christ, prepared by us, written not with ink but with the Spirit of the loving God, not on tablets of stone but on tablets of human hearts" (II Corinthians 3:2-3). Amen.

Now invite the group to create valentines using the Bible verses as well as the craft supplies.

Follow the crafting of valentines with the making of valentine pizzas.

While the pizzas are baking, clean up the craft area. Set out plates, cups, napkins, forks, salad, and beverages. Enjoy.

Lent: Pancake Tuesday

A pancake race, followed by a meal of pancakes, marks the beginning of Lent.

Mark 1:13: "And he was in the wilderness forty days, tempted by Satan; and he was with the wild beasts; and the angels ministered to him."

Preparations

Foods: pancakes; syrup; butter or margarine; fruit salad; sausage or bacon (optional); beverages; and candy bars (for prizes)

Materials: a bell; four or five small, lightweight frying pans; monk's robe (optional); plates; cups; napkins; knives; forks; and spoons

At Home:
This event or a breakfast, luncheon, or dinner, is usually held on the Tuesday before Ash Wednesday. However, a pancake race would be a creative addition to any occasion when pancakes are served.

Make plans for cooking the pancakes and recruit cooks. Pancakes can be cooked at church or made at home and reheated. For a group consisting of children and adults, plan on four to five four-inch pancakes per person.

Volunteers can bring bowls of fruit salad or fruit to be added to a group salad. Sausage and bacon, while not necessary, are often served with pancakes. Beverages might include orange juice, milk, coffee, and tea. Organize a crew to help with set up and clean up.

Pancake races are to be held before the meal. Find a good sport to play the role of the bellringer, usually a man. If by any chance you have a robe that resembles a monk's robe, coax the bellringer into wearing it.

Decide where the race is to be held and the route the racers will take. Outdoors works well, weather permitting. If the race is to be held indoors, the route can weave from room to room, run the length of a corridor, or wrap around the outskirts of a fellowship hall. Consider safety, and design a route that will minimize the danger of tripping.

Candy bars make fine prizes for the winners.

Before the Gathering:
Set serving and dining tables and put out butter, syrup, fruit, plates, cups, napkins, knives, forks, and spoons. Prepare beverages.

Cooks will want to begin to cook the pancakes and bacon or sausage, all of which can be kept warm in the oven. If the pancakes were cooked at home, set them in the oven to reheat.

You will need cooked pancakes to place in the frying pans for the pancake race.

Gathering for Pancakes

The bellringer can welcome the group and invite everyone to be seated. Begin the program with a history of Lent and Pancake Tuesday:

27

Pancake Tuesday is a delightful custom that dates back hundreds of years. Also called Shrove Tuesday, this day the shriving bell was rung, summoning Christians to church to confess their sins before the start of Lent the next day, Ash Wednesday.

Taken from the forty-days that Jesus spent in the wilderness before his temptation by Satan, Lent is the forty-day period that precedes Easter Sunday. The name is derived from the Anglo-Saxon *lencten,* which means "spring."

In years gone by, Lent was observed by certain days of fasting and other days when specific foods, usually meat, were not permitted. Eggs, butter and other fats, and milk were completely forbidden during Lent. Since fats were not to be consumed, the name *Fat Tuesday,* or *Mardi Gras* in French, became synonymous with Shrove Tuesday. Because pancakes use milk and eggs as well as fat, a meal of pancakes was an excellent way to use up these ingredients before Ash Wednesday. Thus one more name for Shrove Tuesday, Pancake Tuesday.

Since it was the last day before the austere period of Lent, Pancake Tuesday became a day of festive frivolity. One popular custom was the pancake race. The shriving bell became known as the pancake bell. Housewives, with a freshly cooked pancake in a frying pan, would gather in the town square when they heard the bell. The women then rushed from the square to the church, tossing the pancake in the air three times before reaching their destination. The bellringer ate the winner's pancake and then gave her a kiss.

Tell the group that they will now witness an authentic pancake race. Men and children will enjoy watching the women race, or they can be invited to race too.

Explain the race route. Introduce the bellringer, and send him to the place where the race is to finish. Those not racing may want to wait at the finish line as well. If the race is to be held in a fellowship hall, all will have a good view from where they are.

Choose as many racers as you have frying pans. Several races may be necessary to include all who want to race. If your group is reluctant to participate, some lighthearted coercion may be needed.

Hand a frying pan with a pancake in it to each racer. If the bellringer is in sight, he can ring his bell or you can signal the start of the race.

Remember that the bellringer eats the pancake of the winner and then gives her a kiss. A prize of a candy bar, as well as hearty congratulations, can reward all racers.

By now the kitchen helpers should have the pancakes and other foods ready to serve. Ask the bellringer to ring his bell and gather everyone back together. Perhaps he would say the blessing:

Holy Father,
   As has been a tradition for hundreds of years, we will feast on pancakes before Lent begins. Bless this food to our nourishment.

During this Lenten season, open our minds and hearts to the death and joyful Resurrection of your Son, Jesus Christ. Amen.

Let the feast begin!

World Communion Sunday: Bread from Many Lands

Partake of the daily bread of many lands in an international celebration of Holy Communion.

I Corinthians 10:17: "Because there is one bread, we who are many are one body, for we all partake of the one bread."

Preparations

Foods: international breads; grape juice; beverages (for coffee hour)

Materials: Holy Communion: baskets or communion bread tray; cloth napkins; communion goblets or individual communion cups
Coffee Hour: tablecloth and other decorations; index cards for labels; plates; cups; napkins

At Home:
World Communion Sunday, the first Sunday in October, is celebrated each year by churches throughout the world. The international significance of this occasion can be enhanced by serving bread from many lands for communion bread.

Three or four weeks before World Communion Sunday, ask for volunteers to bake or purchase international breads. A notice can be placed in the bulletin and an eye-catching poster, perhaps with magazine pictures of breads, will help publicize this event. You may want to personally ask individuals for breads, especially ask persons you know who bake a special type of bread. If baking is not possible, many international breads can be purchased from bakeries. Grocery stores sell tortillas, pita bread, rye bread, French, and Italian bread.

Because only a small amount of bread is needed for communion and each communicant will taste only one kind, a coffee hour following the service gives everyone an opportunity to sample all of the breads. Also, a coffee hour helps children who do not yet participate in communion understand the international significance of World Communion Sunday. Dolls, a tablecloth, flags, or other international artifacts can be used as decorations and will add to the mood of the coffee hour.

Of course, your pastor will want to work with you in planning this communion service.

Before the Gathering:
From each type of bread, cut pieces suitable for communion. Arrange the

bread in baskets or on communion trays. Pour the grape juice in goblets or in individual communion cups for dipping the bread. Put the communion elements on the altar or communion table.

Prepare a list of the breads to be served and give it to your pastor or lay leader.

If you have planned a coffee hour, decorate the tables, put out napkins, plates, and cups, and prepare beverages. The remainder of the breads can be sliced and arranged on serving plates. Labels next to the plates will identify each type of bread.

Gathering for an International Holy Communion

At some point in the service, the pastor or lay leader should explain that the communion breads are representative of many lands. The list of breads to be served can then be read.

If your church has a children's sermon or sharing time, the breads can be shown to the children and the celebration of World Communion Sunday explained.

If there is to be a coffee hour following the service, this should be announced and the congregation warmly invited.

The following benediction is especially appropriate for World Communion Sunday:

> Jesus said: "I am the bread of life." Paul tells us: "Because there is one bread, we who are many are one body." Go in peace to serve the Lord in communion with your brothers and sisters throughout the world. In the name of the Father and of the Son and of the Holy Spirit. Amen.

All Souls' Tea: A Time for Remembrance

Share recipes, heirlooms, and memories of loved ones at a special tea in their honor.

Romans 8:38-39: "For I am convinced that neither death, nor life, nor angels, nor rulers, nor things present, nor things to come, nor powers, nor height, nor depth, nor anything else in all creation, will be able to separate us from the love of God in Christ Jesus our Lord."

Preparations

Foods: teas and coffees, a variety of blends; foods suitable for a tea; cream; milk; sugar; lemon

Materials: pretty tablecloths; centerpiece; index cards for labels and recipes; pens or markers; tea and coffee pots; creamers and sugar bowls; plates; cups; napkins; forks; and spoons

At Home:

The All Souls' Tea is a special time to reminisce and pay respect to loved ones who have died. A wonderful way to make conversation about the departed is through objects that belonged to them. A war medal, pocket knife, a pair of gloves, a wedding ring, a game board, a quilt, photographs, and even letters provide a focal point of interest and conversation.

Publicize this event early and often in order that everyone will have time to search for heirlooms, photos, and other keepsakes. Also, ask those attending to bring favorite family foods such as finger sandwiches, small cakes, or cheese straws that are suitable for a tea. Encourage everyone to bring copies of the recipes to accompany the food.

Select a variety of teas and coffees to be served. Of course you will need a number of coffee and tea pots.

Contact volunteers who will assist you with the program.

Before the Gathering:

Prepare serving and display tables.

Assign helpers to guide people to the display tables and label the items brought, assist in arranging foods and recipes on the serving table, brew teas and coffees, and serve the beverages.

Gathering for an All Souls' Day Tea

After all objects and foods have been placed on the tables, invite everyone to be seated. Begin the program:

All Souls' Day, which follows All Saints' Day on the Christian calendar, is a holy day that remembers and honors our departed loved ones.

Next, ask the group to listen to the comforting words of Romans 8:38-39.

After the reading, thank the group for bringing their objects, foods, and recipes. Tell them that as the refreshments are served, they are to enjoy looking over the display tables and sharing memories with one another. Ask them to pray with you as you say this old benediction:

"The LORD bless you and keep you;
the LORD make his face to shine upon you, and be
    gracious to you;
the Lord lift up his countenance upon you, and give you
    peace" (Numbers 6:24-26) Amen.

Cherish the refreshments and the memories.

IV. STEWARDS OF GOD'S BOUNTY

Workday Group Soup: "Striving Side by Side for the Faith"

The aroma of simmering soup makes for happy workers.

Philippians 1:27: "You are standing firm in one spirit, striving side by side with one mind for the faith of the gospel."

Preparations

Foods: Workday Group Soup (Recipe Collection); bread; butter or margarine; jam or jelly; dessert; beverages

Materials: large pot for cooking soup; ladle; bowls; plates; bread baskets; napkins; cups; knives; forks; and spoons

At Home:
Almost all churches have workdays from time to time, whether they be for cleaning the church, painting the Sunday school rooms, or sewing for the bazaar. For the meal at this gathering, everyone is asked to bring a vegetable to add to a soup stock. Workday Group Soup not only makes a delicious meal but it symbolically reinforces Paul's words to the church at Philippi that are quoted above.

You may want to use this thought and verse in the publicity for the workday. Be sure to request that each participant or family bring a vegetable to add to the soup. Beverages, bread, and dessert can be provided by the workday committee.

The workday should begin at least two hours before you plan to serve the soup so that it will have plenty of time to simmer.

Prepare the soup stock according to the recipe.

Before the Gathering:
Pour the soup stock into the pot and begin to heat.

Gathering for Workday Group Soup

As the workers arrive be sure that they are directed to the kitchen to add their vegetables to the soup.

As the soup simmers, put out the breads, butter and jam, beverages, and desserts. Set up the serving and dining tables.

Before the soup is served, ask the group to gather for grace. You may want to add a few words about the day's work project:

Heavenly Father,
Many vegetables make good soup and many hands make light work as we strive together, side by side, for the faith of the gospel.
We pray in Jesus' name. Amen.

As the soup is served remind the workers that it is indeed soup made by the group!

Tray Favors: "Greet One Another with a Holy Kiss"

Send greetings from your church to patients in hospitals and nursing homes.

Romans 16:16: "Greet one another with a holy kiss."

Preparations

Foods: Hershey's Kisses

Materials: Plastic wrap; curling ribbon; 3-by-5 unlined index cards; scissors; markers or pens

At Home:
Each tray favor will take four Hershey's kisses. Purchase enough candy to make the desired number of favors and an extra bag to fortify chocolate loving workers. There are about 80 kisses in a 14-ounce bag.
Tear plastic wrap into squares.
Cut index cards into quarter sections to measure 1½-by-2½ inches. Punch a hole for ribbon at one end.

Before the Gathering:
Set out the materials for making the favors.

Gathering to Make Tray Favors

Before making the tray favors, say a few words about the gesture of the kiss in biblical days:

Perhaps the most notorious kiss in the Bible is the kiss given to Jesus by Judas in the Garden of Gethsemane. Not only did Judas betray Jesus, but he did this with a gesture that expressed love. The kiss, usually extended as a greeting, was exchanged between both family members and comrades.
Since early Christians often exchanged kisses upon greeting, these kisses became a sign of Christian brotherhood. Paul writes in his letter to the Romans: "Greet one another with a holy kiss" (Romans 16:16).

Tell the group that they will now be sending greetings made of candy kisses. Demonstrate how to construct the favors:

Put four kisses in the center of a piece of plastic wrap and secure with a length of ribbon about 15 inches long. Write "Greetings from
_____ ." on a tag and attach it to the ribbon.
       your church's name
Tie the ribbon with a bow and curl the ends if you like.

As the group starts to work, tell them that sampling is permissible. Close the gathering with a prayer:

Heavenly Father,
    Bless these greetings from our church and bestow your peace on those who receive them. Amen.

The tray favors can be given to a nursing home or hospital. Meals on Wheels, senior citizen centers, and shelters are also often appreciative of tray favors.

Bread for the Birds: "Even the Sparrow Finds a Home"

Just as God remembers the sparrow that falls, decorating a tree with pine-cone bird feeders is a thoughtful way to care for the birds that nest in your churchyard.

Psalm 84:3: Even the sparrow finds a home,
        and the swallow a nest for herself,
        where she may lay her young,
    at your altars, O LORD of hosts,
        my King and my God.

Preparations

Foods: peanut butter; jelly; bread; juice

Materials: pine cones (one per person); birdseed; string or yarn; newspaper; pan; knives; cups; napkins

At Home:
    Find medium size to large size pine cones. These will be covered in peanut butter and rolled in birdseed to create bird feeders.
    Select a tree on your church property with low branches where the bird feeders can be hung. Birds will be less reluctant to visit the tree if it isn't too near a building.
    Prepare peanut-butter-and-jelly sandwiches for refreshments. If the sandwiches are made more than a few hours ahead of time, you can keep the jelly from leaking through the bread by spreading peanut butter on each piece of bread and the jelly in the center.

Before the Gathering:
    Cover a table with newspaper. Pour the birdseed into a pan and put it on the table along with the peanut butter, knives, and string.
    Prepare beverages.

Gathering to Feed the Birds

Before work on the bird feeders begins, say a word about birds in the Bible:

Birds are mentioned throughout the Bible beginning with the story of creation in Genesis. Sea gulls, doves, ravens, storks, hens, owls, sparrows, swallows, and eagles are among the birds mentioned by name. In biblical times, bats, which we now know are mammals, were thought to be birds.

Birds play an important role in several Bible stories. Noah first sends a raven out of the ark to see if the flood waters have subsided. Next he sends a dove. When the dove returns with a freshly plucked olive leaf in her mouth, Noah knows that the waters have indeed subsided (Genesis 8:6-12). At the baptism of Jesus the dove is a sign of the Holy Spirit: "And the Holy Spirit descended on him in bodily form like a dove" (Luke 3:22).

Birds are used to help explain the ways of God. Isaiah 31:5 says: "Like birds hovering overhead, so the LORD of hosts will protect Jerusalem." In Matthew, Jesus asks: "Look at the birds of the air; they neither sow nor reap nor gather into barns, and yet your heavenly Father feeds them. Are you not of more value than they?" (Matthew 6:26). Jesus reminds us that even the ways of the birds are controlled by God: "Are not two sparrows sold for a penny? Yet not one of them will fall to the ground apart from your Father" (Matthew 10:29). Jesus continues by saying that we are of more value than many sparrows.

Although the Bible tells us that humans are more valuable than birds, God wants us to respect them as creatures of his creation. Listen to Psalm 84, verse 3:

> Even the sparrow finds a home,
>   and the swallow a nest for herself,
>   where she may lay her young,
>   at your altars, O LORD of hosts,
>   my King and my God.

These lines speak of birds at God's altars, possibly birds nesting near a temple.

Tell the group that today they are going to honor the birds that nest near their church. Show a sample bird feeder and explain how it is made.

Disperse the group to make the bird feeders. Young children will need help, as peanut butter can be quite messy. After the pine cones have been spread with peanut butter, roll them in bird seed. String tied around the pine cone will form a hanger.

After any messy hands have been washed, have the group carry their birdfeeders to the chosen tree.

When the bird feeders have been hung, offer a prayer for the birds:

Creator God,
    Just as the psalm speaks of sparrows and swallows that nest at your altars, we dedicate this tree to the birds that grace our churchyard. Bless this food to their nourishment. Amen.

Invite everyone back inside for peanut-butter-and-jelly sandwiches, a snack, reminiscent no doubt, of the treat just left for the birds.

Hospitality to Strangers:
"Some Have Entertained Angels Without Knowing It"

Hosting Christians from another church or organization is fun with The Mingling Angels Game and an easy meal of hot dogs.

Hebrews 13:2: "Do not neglect to show hospitality to strangers, for by doing that some have entertained angels without knowing it."

Preparations

Foods: hot dogs; buns; condiments; side salads; desserts; beverages

Materials: name tags and pens; plates; cups; napkins; and forks
game: construction, shelf, or computer paper (halos); poster board, shelf, or computer paper (poster); tape; scissors; markers

At Home:
Extend hospitality to other Christians by hosting a workshop, visiting youth group, or ecumenical luncheon.
Appoint helpers who will prepare the hot dogs and assist with setting up and managing the welcoming, serving, and dining tables.
Your host group should be asked to bring side salads, beverages, and desserts.
This event features The Mingling Angels Game. Use paper to create halos. Cut paper in strips measuring 1½-x-24 inches. In the center of one side, print or draw a Christian symbol. Below is a list of 25 symbols. Repeat symbols if your group is larger than 25 people:

ship	cross	grapes	dove	staff
fish	crown	butterfly	flames	serpent
bread	angel	candle	heart	tablet
cup	rainbow	triangle	lamb	Bible
coin	bell	star	nails	water

Do not tape the halos into circlets until fitting them onto each individual at the gathering.
Also, make a poster explaining the rules of the game:

The Mingling Angels Game

Object of the Game: To mingle with other angels by asking questions to determine what Christian symbol is printed on your halo.

How to Play: Begin by asking, Is it animal? Vegetable? Mineral? Ethereal? Is it large? and so on.
All answers must be either yes or no.
Take turns by asking each other two questions, then switch partners.

Finishing: The game will end when all angels have guessed their symbol.

Before the Gathering:
Ask helpers to prepare the tables. The welcoming table needs paper halos (face down), tape, pens, and name tags. Display the poster near the table.
Either the serving or dining tables need cups, plates, napkins, and forks. Put someone in charge of arranging the salads, beverages, and desserts on the serving table as people bring them.
A kitchen crew will be needed to heat the hot dogs and buns.

Gathering to Entertain Angels

As members of your host group arrive, ask them to take their contribution to the serving table and then proceed to the welcoming table. Guide all guests to the welcoming table.
Everyone will be fitted with a paper halo, secured by tape, and told that a symbol of the Church is printed on it. Ask all angels to read the game rules and then begin.
When the game is finished, ask the blessing:

> Universal God,
> We know that we are one in the body of Christ and as we come together today we are reminded of our relationship to one another. Bless this food and this fellowship and let us be mindful to "show hospitality to strangers, for by doing that some have entertained angels without knowing it." Amen.

Invite the angels that you are entertaining to be first in line!

A Salad Buffet: "You Shall Be Like a Watered Garden"

Everyone relishes a good salad bar and the local food bank always needs contributions of canned food.

Isaiah 58:11: The LORD will guide you continually,
        and satisfy your needs in parched places,
        and make your bones strong;
    and you shall be like a watered garden,
        like a spring of water,
    whose waters never fail.

Preparations

Foods: items for a salad bar; beverages; contributions of canned foods

Materials: large box or hamper for canned foods; bowls or plates; cups; and napkins

At Home:
Combine fellowship with mission by sponsoring a garden salad bar and a canned food drive. Most food banks need contributions of canned food, especially in the spring and summer months. Contact the food bank to learn their guidelines and particular needs. You may wish to tour the facility and report to your group or you might ask a person from the food bank program to be a guest speaker at the buffet.

The ingredients for the salad bar may be prepared by one group or provided by all who attend.

Before the Gathering:
Arrange serving and dining tables with plates, napkins, cups, and forks. Line up the salad items, beginning with the greens and ending with the dressings.

Place the box or hamper in a convenient spot to collect the canned goods as the group arrives.

Gathering for a Garden Buffet

Welcome everyone, introduce the guest speaker if you have one, and explain that the program will follow the salad buffet.
Ask the blessing:

Holy Creator,
We are stewards of your world and its bounty. Please guide us to the caring and generous paths in life. You have made us "like a watered garden" that we may provide much. Thank you for all your good gifts. Amen.

After the buffet, begin the program:

In the Holy Land, water is a precious commodity, and the cultivation of a piece of ground requires water.

The Old Testament people appreciated the sustenance and refreshment of a garden. In those ancient times the best location for a garden was near a source of water such as a stream or spring. When this was not possible, a well might be dug or a cistern built to catch rain water.

In this arid climate water became a symbol. The book of Jeremiah tells of "living waters" (Jeremiah 2:3) and that trust in the Lord is like being a tree planted near waters of a stream (Jeremiah 17:7-8). The words of Isaiah speak of abundance as "like a watered garden" (Isaiah 58:11) and scarcity as a "garden without water" (Isaiah 1:30).

Biblical gardens were often walled with stone or hedges. They were filled with flowering trees, fruit trees, shrubs, vegetables, herbs, spices, and flowers.

The Hebrews loved their gardens and saw them as a sign of a happy home (Psalm 128:33) and as a good place for prayer, meditation, and even burial. Two famous biblical gardens are the Garden of Gethsemane, where Jesus went for spiritual retreat, and the Garden of Joseph of Arimathea, where Jesus was buried.

Thank the group for sharing fruits of a watered garden in both the salad buffet and their donations to the foodbank.

Next, tell of the needs of your local food bank or introduce your guest speaker.

Cookie Tasting and Trade: A Thank You to Community Helpers

Deserving community helpers will know how much they are appreciated when they receive plates of homemade cookies.

I Corinthians 10:31: "So, whether you eat or drink, or whatever you do, do everything for the glory of God."

Preparations

Foods: six dozen homemade cookies per participant; beverages

Materials: photocopies of cookie recipes; disposable plates; plastic wrap; curling ribbon; scissors; labels or tags; cups; and napkins

At Home:
In publicizing this event, make clear that each participant needs to bring at least six dozen cookies and photocopies of his or her recipe. This event works well any time of the year, but is most fitting at Christmastime. Plates of homemade cookies will be packaged and delivered to community helpers, and along with tasking cookies, each participant will take a variety of cookies and recipes home.

The disposable plates, plastic wrap, curling ribbon, and labels or tags will be used to package the cookies.

Before the Gathering:
Set up a table for packaging the cookies and on it place the plates, wrap, ribbon, scissors, and labels. Another table will be needed for refreshments.

Prepare beverages and set out cups and napkins.

Gathering to Taste and Trade

As the participants arrive ask that the cookies be placed on the packaging table. When it is time to begin, offer this prayer:

Gracious God,
Today we have gathered to make plates of cookies for our community workers. We are reminded of Paul's words: "So, whether you eat or drink, or whatever you do, do everything for the glory of God." Thank you for those who work to make our community whole. Amen.

39

While the cookies are being packaged, decide with the group where the plates should be delivered. Keep in mind fire, police, and rescue stations; shelters; health clinics; school offices; the library; and social service organizations. Each plate should hold three dozen cookies and be wrapped in plastic, labeled, and tied with ribbon.

Make several plates for the refreshment table. Then divide the rest of the cookies among the group.

Serve the beverages and invite everyone to sit around the refreshment table to taste the cookies from many kitchens.

V. FOODS OF THE HOLY LAND

Pistachio Nuts and Almonds: "Choice Fruits of the Land"

A scrap of muslin and a snip of string turn pistachio nuts and almonds into a biblical surprise.

Genesis 43:11: "Then their father Israel said to them, 'If it must be so, then do this: take some of the choice fruits of the land in your bags, and carry down to the man as a present—a little balm and a little honey, gum, resin, pistachio nuts, and almonds.' "

Try this activity as an interesting introduction to a meeting.

Preparations

Foods: pistachio nuts and almonds

Materials: 6-inch squares of muslin; 15-inch lengths of string

At Home:
Purchase nuts with or without shells and plan on a scant ¼ cup per person.
Cut the muslin and the string. Portion out the nuts by placing them in the center of the cloth square. Tie with the string to form a bag.

Before the Gathering
As each person arrives, hand him or her a nut bag, but ask that it not be opened yet.

Gathering for Choice Fruits

Open with a simple prayer from Psalms:

> Lord,
> "Let the words of my mouth and the
> meditation of my heart
> be acceptable to you,
> O LORD, my rock and my redeemer."
> Amen. (Psalm 19:14)

Tell the group that inside their bags are "choice fruits of the land." Invite them to open the bags. While they are snacking, offer the biblical background:

Although native trees of Palestine, the almond and pistachio are so favored that they have been cultivated for over 4,000 years.

The almond, considered a branch of the rose family, flowers with pink blossoms in January. The almond nuts and oil are highly prized. The Bible tells us that an almond rod bursting forth with blossoms was used as proof that Aaron was God's choice to be the first high priest of Israel (Numbers 17:8).

The pistachio, often referred to as the "green almond," is valued for its flavorful nut and the green coloring used as a dye.

Along with the almond, the pistachio was considered one of the "choice fruits of the land" as we read in the story of Joseph.

Conclude by reading Genesis 43:11.

A Treasure Hunt: "Like Treasure Hidden in a Field"

Everyone loves a treasure hunt!

Matthew 13:44: "The kingdom of heaven is like treasure hidden in a field, which someone found and hid; then in his joy he goes and sells all that he has and buys that field."

Preparations

Foods: small boxes of raisins; Bit O' Honey candy; carob candy; pistachio nuts; almonds or candy with almonds; mints

Materials: sandwich bags or plastic wrap; bags for collecting treasure; paper; pencils; a treasure chest

At Home:
Children love treasure hunts, but adults, too, will have a good time with this activity.

Determine where the treasure hunt will be held. The parable speaks of

41

treasure hidden in a field so a grassy spot outdoors is fitting, but also choose an indoor location in the event of inclement weather.

Purchase foods to be hidden. The treats listed above are related to Holy Land foods. You may be able to think of others. Estimate the number of people you expect to attend and allow for five or more items to be found per person.

Any loose foods can be placed in plastic wrap or sandwich bags and tied with ribbon or yarn.

Decorate a shoe box to be a treasure chest or find a pretty box to serve as one.

Before the Gathering:

Hide the treasure before anyone is due to arrive. If children will be arriving near the hiding spot, you may need a sentry to stand guard. Keep a sample of each type of treat to show to the group before the hunt begins.

Gathering for a Treasure Hunt

After welcoming the group, offer this prayer:

> Father Eternal,
>   As Christians, may we lay up for ourselves treasures in heaven and not on earth, for where our treasure is, there will our heart be also. We pray in Jesus' name. Amen.

Next, pose the following question: If you uncovered a treasure chest in your garden, what would you like to find inside it?

After the answers are recorded, ask that they be put in the treasure chest. Young children may need some help recording their answers.

Shake the treasure chest, pose the question again, and with a dramatic flair, read the answers. Use the answers to lead into a discussion of the idea of treasure in the Bible:

The Bible warns us that earthly treasure will not last, but the treasures of God will last forever. Jesus tells us: "Do not store up for yourselves treasures on earth, where moth and rust consume and where thieves break in and steal; but store up for yourselves treasures in heaven" (Matthew 6:19-20). In fact, Jesus uses hidden treasure to describe the kingdom of heaven: "The kingdom of heaven is like treasure hidden in a field, which someone found and hid; then in his joy he goes and sells all that he has and buys that field" (Matthew 13:44). Jesus wants his listeners to understand that we must be completely dedicated to the Christian faith.

Tell the group that to help them remember the parable of treasure hidden in a field, they will now take part in a treasure hunt. Show a sample of each treat and briefly explain how it is related to a food of the Holy Land.

Give each treasure hunter a bag. Lead the group to the field and with a signal such as a bell or whistle, begin the hunt.

Treasures may be eaten on the spot.

Lentils: A Birthright for a Bowl of Soup

Can the men in your church cook as well as Jacob?

Genesis 25:34: "Then Jacob gave Esau bread and lentil stew, and he ate and drank, and rose and went his way. Thus Esau despised his birthright."

Preparations

Foods: Lentil Stew (Recipe Collection); Flatbread (Recipe Collection); salad (optional); dessert (optional); beverages

Materials: soup pot; ladle; bowls; cups; napkins; forks; and spoons

At Home:
Since Jacob was a good cook and made the lentil stew he traded to Esau, this is an especially fitting program for a men's group.
Bake Flatbread or purchase pita bread from the grocery store.
Although it does not take long to cook, the stew tastes best if made a day or two ahead of time and allowed to mellow.
Salad and dessert, while optional, make for a complete meal. Salad might be Bible Garden Salad (Recipe Collection) and dessert, St. John's Brownies (Recipe Collection).

Before the Gathering:
Set up as many dining tables as you think you will need. Put salad plates, forks and spoons, and napkins on each table.
The stew may be served from the stove or a soup tureen. Begin to reheat the soup. Place the flatbread on the table with the salad and dessert if you are serving them. Either set up a serving area for beverages or bring them to the table when the meal is served.

Gathering for Lentil Stew

Ask that everyone take a place around the table (or tables). Announce that the menu consists of foods prevalent in biblical days: Lentil Stew and Flatbread. If you are serving salad and dessert, mention these too.
Next give some information about the consumption of lentils and bread in the Bible:

The lentil has been cultivated in the Holy Land for thousands of years. Classified as a legume, the seeds are high in protein and carbohydrates. In Bible days the lentil was usually cooked as a soup, pottage, or stew. Esau is ravenous with hunger in the story of Jacob and Esau. In fact he is so hungry that he trades his birthright to his brother, Jacob, in exchange for a bowl of lentil stew. Read Genesis 25:29-34.
The Bible also tells of lentils being combined with other ingredients to make a bread (Ezekiel 4:9).
In biblical days, bread was a part of almost every meal. A very flat bread

43

was especially useful at a time when forks and spoons were not in common use. The bread was broken and a piece was used to scoop up soup or stew. This is translated "sop" in the King James Version, "morsel" in the Revised Standard Version, and simply "piece of bread" in the New Revised Standard Version.

As a sign of hospitality, the master of the feast would dip the sop from a bowl in the center of the table and hand it to each of his guests. The sop plays an important part in the betrayal of Jesus. Read John 13:21-30.

Both readings have spoken of food used in a betrayal. Yet throughout the Bible there are many pleasant references to food. Ecclesiastes 3:13 tells us, "It is God's gift that all should eat and drink and take pleasure in all their toil."

The time has come for your group to eat and drink. Challenge them to eat their stew with a sop of Flatbread. For cowards, spoons have been placed on the table.

Before the meal is served, say a blessing:

God of our fathers and mothers,
Just as your children, the Hebrews, partook of these foods long ago, we eat them now. We ask you to bless this food.
We pray in the name of Jesus, the bread of life from heaven. Amen.

By the time the meal is finished, your group should have a greater appreciation for the invention of silverware.

A Shepherds' Picnic: "I Am the Good Shepherd"

Bread, cheese, and a chance meeting with two shepherds give picnickers a taste of shepherds' life in biblical days.

John 10:14: "I am the good shepherd, I know my own and my own know me."

Preparations

Foods: Flatbread (Recipe Collection) or pita bread; a variety of cheeses; grapes; dates; raisins; and dried figs

Materials: baskets for carrying and serving food; picnic blankets; paper napkins and plates; costumes for two shepherds (optional)

At Home:
Bake Flatbread or purchase pita bread from the grocery store. For convenience you may prefer to prepare the food baskets at home, placing bread, grapes, cheeses, and dried fruits in separate baskets. Preslicing the cheese eliminates the need for knives. Store paper napkins and plates in another basket.

44

Recruit two willing souls to play the part of the shepherds. Since both men and women worked as shepherds in biblical times, your players may be male or female. Give them a photocopy of the "Shepherds' Dialogue."* Request that they arrive early for the event so they can be in place when the picnic begins.

Although costumes are not necessary, they add an authentic touch. Shawls, table cloths, bathrobes, or large pieces of cloth will serve as the shepherd's cloak. A pouch of cloth or leather can be the shepherd's bag. Sandals and a staff will complete the costume.

Choose a spot for the picnic. This activity works well on a church lawn, in a retreat setting, at a park, or in a backyard. In cold or inclement weather, the picnic can be held in a fellowship hall, you may choose to depart for the picnic from another location in your church.

Before the Gathering:
The shepherds should put on their costumes and wait for the group at the picnic spot.

Gathering for a Shepherds' Picnic

When everyone has arrived, call the group together. Hand the baskets and picnic cloths to several picnickers and have everyone follow you to the picnic spot. When you arrive exclaim how fortunate you are to have chanced upon real shepherds! Ask the picnickers to be seated and listen to the shepherds' conversation:

Shepherds' Dialogue

SHEPHERD ONE: . . . And then Elizabeth told me that she had heard of thieves about the hills.

SHEPHERD TWO: Where did you see her?

SHEPHERD ONE: At the well. She told me that she just let her hired man go because he was careless with the sheep.

SHEPHERD TWO: She's a good shepherdess. I know it upsets her to lose any sheep.

SHEPHERD ONE: You were lucky to get your staff around that lamb yesterday. That was a dangerous climb.

SHEPHERD TWO: It's a good thing we moved to greener pastures today. By the way, did you hear wolves howling last night?

SHEPHERD ONE: Yes, and it worries me because it's lambing season.

SHEPHERD TWO: Let's get the flock counted and in the sheepfold early tonight. We have ewes about to deliver.

SHEPHERD ONE: Ho! Plenty of fresh milk and cheese soon. The Lord has blessed us.

SHEPHERD TWO:	Speaking of food, I'm ready to eat.
SHEPHERD ONE:	So is your favorite lamb. Here he comes to sniff your pouch.
SHEPHERD TWO:	Amazing creatures, sheep. They not only know the sound of their shepherd's voice, but this one knows when it's lunchtime.

When the shepherds' dialogue is finished, invite the shepherds to join you. Next, read the words of Jesus from John 10:1-15.

After the reading, lead the group in the Twenty-third Psalm as a prayer before the meal. Following the psalm, pass the baskets. Enjoy the shepherds' picnic.

Scripture Cake: "By the Encouragement of the Scriptures"

No Christian food book would be complete without this recipe.

Romans 15:4: "For whatever was written in former days was written for our instruction, so that by steadfastness and by the encouragement of the scriptures we might have hope."

Preparations

Food: Scripture Cake (Recipe Collection); beverages

Materials: Bibles (brought by the group); plates; cups; napkins; and forks

At Home:
  In publicizing this gathering, ask everyone to bring along a Bible that has special significance such as a family Bible, a Bible written in a different language, a favorite translation, or one carried in a wedding.
  Bake the cake. If you are anticipating a large group, you may need several cakes.
  Make photocopies of the Scripture Cake recipe* to pass out to the group.

Before the Gathering:
  Cut the cake and arrange it on a serving plate. Prepare beverages. You may want a separate table for displaying the Bibles.

Gathering for Scripture Cake

Begin this event by reading Romans 15:4.
  When the reading is finished, show the Bible that you chose to bring and explain why it is special to you. In turn, ask the rest of the group to say a word about the Bibles they brought.

46

After this is finished, ask everyone to join you in prayer:

God of the Old and New Covenant,
  You have given us your holy scriptures.
As we read and study them, enlighten, encourage,
and instruct us so that we may be steadfast in
faith. We pray in the name of Christ Jesus. Amen.

Announce that in keeping with the theme of the scriptures, the refreshment is appropriately named Scripture Cake. Pass out copies of the recipe. Give a touch of background information:

This is an old New England recipe. In days gone by homemakers had to look up the citations to find the ingredients to be used, unlike this recipe, where they are indicated in parentheses.

There are many versions of the recipe since some of the foods could be interpreted in different ways. For example, Jeremiah 6:20 speaks of sweet cane, which could be either sugar or molasses. The recipe also called for some knowledge of cake baking since some of the passages, such as Judges 5:25, list more than one ingredient. The cook had to decide if she should add butter, milk, or water. Scripture Cake tested a woman's cake baking skills as well as encouraged her to use her Bible.

Serve the cake and the beverages. If you have set up a display table, the Bibles can be placed on it for all to examine.

Food in the Wilderness: Bean Pod or Bug?

After discussing what John the Baptist really ate in the wilderness, treat everyone to St. John's Brownies.

Mark 1:6: "Now John was clothed in camel's hair, with a leather belt around his waist, and he ate locusts and wild honey."

Preparations

Foods: St. John's Brownies (Recipe Collection); beverages

Materials: locust insect (photograph, facsimile, or real bug); carob powder; cups; and napkins

At Home:
The discussion of the wilderness food will stir the curiosity of any age group. The carob treats will give all a pleasant taste of a Holy Land food.
Find a reference book with photographs of locust insects, purchase a plastic insect, or search for a real bug! According to biblical scholars, the locust is similar to the grasshopper.

Locating the carob powder will be more pleasant. Carob powder, necessary for the discussion as well as the brownies, may be purchased at large chain grocery stores, health food stores, or gourmet shops. If any of these stores has a bakery or confectionary, you might find other carob foods to sample such as carob-covered raisins or St. John's carob bread.

After locating the carob powder, bake the St. John's Brownies.

Before the Gathering
Prepare the platter of brownies and the beverages and set out the napkins and cups.

Have the locust props at hand.

Gathering for Wilderness Food

Greet all and open with the story of John the Baptist in the wilderness (Mark 1:1-11). Then give this background:

John the Baptist seems to be a man so filled with a spiritual mission that the simple comforts of home and bed, cooked meals, and a change of clothing were of little importance. The Bible account tells that John ate honey and locusts in the wilderness. The question is: What are locusts? (Hold up the bug and the carob).

Bible scholars argue that John might have eaten either the locust insect or the locust bean. Maybe he ate both.

The locust, or carob tree, is a widely branching tree of medium height native to Syria and Palestine. An evergreen with glossy leaves, the red blossoms grow into long pods or husks filled with beans. A single tree may produce up to one thousand pounds of pods in a season. For thousands of years, the pods have been used as a sweet, nutritious animal fodder.

The prodigal son was thought to have eaten carob husks in his desperation and poverty (Luke 15:16). John the Baptist may have partaken of the tree's fruit as he searched for sustenance in the wilderness.

Although carob pods and beans were food for the poor in biblical times, today carob powder, made from the ground dried beans, is a popular health food.

What about the insect?

The locust insect is depicted in the Bible as both a scourge and a benefit. God sent a swarm of locusts as is told in the book of Exodus (10:1-20). These swarms of locusts can strip all vegetation in an area, travel long distances to attack again, and if plants are scarce, the locusts can become carnivorous. In Revelation 9:4-5, John predicts a future plague of locusts even more terrible than that described in Exodus.

In normal times, locusts are not so threatening. They are identified in Leviticus as edible (11:21-22). A protein source for the poor, locust insects were commonly eaten in biblical days.

Next announce that the biblical food for the day is either locust the plant or locust the bug. Ask the group which they would prefer. (Hold the props up again.)

Most likely the group will be relieved that you have chosen to use carob powder to make St. John's Brownies.

Serve the beverages and enjoy the brownies.

VI. SYMBOLS OF FAITH TO SAVOR

Pretzels: "For We Do Not Know How to Pray"

Retell the legend of the Italian monk who twisted bread dough to create the first pretzel.

Romans 8:26: "We do not know how to pray as we ought, but the very Spirit intercedes with sighs too deep for words."

Preparations

Foods: pretzels; juice

Materials: basket or bowl; cups; and napkins

Before the Gathering:
   Arrange the pretzels in a bowl or basket. Prepare juice.

Gathering for Pretzels

With everyone gathered round, retell the legend of the first pretzel:

A long time ago, around the fifth century, an Italian monk was baking bread in the monastery kitchen. Since it was Lent, the dough he prepared contained no fat or eggs or sugar.

While the bread was in the oven, he sat down to think. The children in his parish did not seem to be learning their prayers. He was worried. He wished that he could think of a clever way to help them learn their prayers as they should. As he thought, he idly rolled a leftover piece of dough between his fingers.

Now in the fifth century children were taught to fold their arms across their chests when they prayed.

As he thought and as he rolled that dough, the clever priest suddenly had an idea. He looped the dough until it looked like folded arms. He put it on a pan and baked it, leaving it in the oven perhaps a little long.

When he took it out of the oven he smiled, "I will call this treat 'pretiola' which means 'little reward,' " he said to himself.

The monk eagerly baked a batch of pretiolas. When the children came to visit, they were delighted with the treat.

Before too long, all the children in the parish began to remember their prayers, and the clever monk baked batch after batch of pretiolas.

After telling the legend, read a verse from the scriptures about prayer: Romans 8:26. In this verse Paul tells the Romans that the Holy Spirit helps us to pray.

Now ask the group to fold their arms across their chests, as the children did in the legend of the pretzel. Say the following prayer:

> Listening God,
> Pretzels rewarded the children of Italy for remembering their prayers. We thank you for pretzels, and we thank you for your Holy Spirit who is with us when we pray. We offer this prayer in Jesus' name. Amen.

Enjoy the pretzels and juice.

Angels: "To Guard You in All Your Ways"

Make any church social event heavenly with a host of ice cream angels.

Psalm 91:11: "For he will command his angels concerning you to guard you in all your ways."

Preparations

Food: Ice Cream Cone Angels (Recipe Collection); beverages

Materials: tablecloth; small plates; napkins; cups; spoons; and small paper doilies

At Home:
Consult the Recipe Collection for the ingredients you will need to make Ice Cream Cone Angels. All foods and supplies may remain packaged until you are setting up for the event.

Plan for the group to sing the first verse of "Angels We Have Heard on High." This may be a cappella or with accompaniment.

You may want helpers to greet, serve, and clear tables.

Before the Gathering:
Assign your helpers to their tasks.

Set up a serving table, with a tablecloth and napkins. You may want dining tables or simply chairs for the group.

Prepare beverages.

Next, create the Ice Cream Cone Angels according to the recipe. Keep ice cream and whipped cream chilled until it is time to serve.

Gathering for an Ice Cream Social

When the group has gathered together, begin the program by singing "Angels We Have Heard on High." Then tell them that they sang this carol because the ice cream social they are attending is a celebration of angels, classic figures throughout the Bible and central to stories that are quite dear to us.

Ask all mortals to bow their heads as the blessing is read from Psalm 103:20-22:

> "Bless the LORD, O you his angels,
>   you mighty ones who do his bidding,
>   obedient to his spoken word.
> Bless the LORD, all his hosts,
>   his ministers that do his will.
> Bless the LORD, all his works,
>   in all places of his dominion.
> Bless the LORD, O my soul." Amen.

With servers in place, invite everyone to line up for an Ice Cream Cone Angel.

The Cross:
"He Humbled Himself and Became Obedient to the Point of Death"

Follow the custom passed down through the ages of marking sweet rolls with the sign of the cross.

Philippians 2:7-8: "And being found in human form, he humbled himself and became obedient to the point of death—even death on a cross."

Preparations

Foods: Easy Hot Cross Buns (Recipe Collection); Believer's Frosting (Recipe Collection) or tubes of white frosting; beverages

Materials: bowls and spoons (for frosting); basket and cloth napkins or tea towel; plates; cups; and napkins

At Home:
Prepare dough for the Easy Hot Cross Buns according to the recipe in the

51

Recipe Collection. The buns may be baked at home and reheated at church or baked at church immediately before the gathering. In many places, especially during Lent, Hot Cross Buns can be purchased from bakeries.

Mix the Believer's Frosting and store it in the refrigerator. If you purchase tubes of white frosting, you will need several tubes.

Before the Gathering:

Prepare beverages and set out plates, cups, and napkins.

The Believer's Frosting should be divided among several bowls with three or four spoons in each bowl. Put the bowls or tubes of frosting on the table.

Plan to bake or reheat the buns so they will be warm when the gathering begins. Just before you ask the group to be seated, wrap the buns in a cloth and place them in a basket.

Gathering for Hot Cross Buns

After greeting the group, tell them that they are about to partake of a treat that dates to ancient times, Hot Cross Buns. Recount the history of these buns:

Every spring in ancient times, sweet rolls were baked in honor of the goddess of spring, Eostre. After the Crucifixion of Jesus, the early Christians worried about eating rolls baked in honor of a pagan goddess. They began to embellish the rolls with a cross made of frosting.

In time, the rolls were brought to Great Britain by the Romans. Soon known as Hot Cross Buns, they were sold by street vendors on Good Friday morning. Their cry "Hot Cross Buns" could be heard up and down the streets and even became a nursery rhyme.

Pause and invite everyone to say the rhyme with you:

> Hot Cross Buns
> How Cross Buns
> One a penny, two a penny,
> Hot Cross Buns.

Superstitions became linked with the buns. Some thought that eating them on Good Friday would prevent a house from catching on fire. Others believed that the buns, ground up and mixed with water, could be used throughout the year for medicinal purposes. Sailors brought the buns to sea to ward off rats from their ships, and farmers hung them in their barns to keep rats away from their fields.

Uncover the buns. Announce that soon these ordinary sweet rolls will become Hot Cross Buns. Demonstrate how to drizzle or squeeze icing onto a bun in the sign of the cross.

Next, read Philippians 2:8.

After the verse, offer this prayer.

Holy God,
As Christians, we celebrate the death and joyful Resurrection of your only son, Jesus. We ask for your blessing as we mark these rolls with the sign of his cross. Amen.

Distribute plates, napkins, and buns. While the buns are being decorated, serve the beverages.

As the Hot Cross Buns are happily consumed, share conversation and fellowship.

Canes: "Your Rod and Your Staff—They Comfort Me"

Today few realize that this Yuletide confection was created in honor of the Christmas shepherds.

Psalm 23:4: "You are with me; your rod and your staff—they comfort me."

Preparations

Foods: candy canes

Materials: a shepherd's staff or a cane

At Home:
This is a good idea for a children's sermon or special Sunday school lesson. Don't forget youth groups and adults who may be surprised to learn of the biblical significance of candy canes.

Locate a shepherd's staff. Perhaps one is part of a shepherd's ensemble in your church's wardrobe collection. If you can't find a staff, a cane with a curved handle will suffice.

Purchase candy canes.

Before the Gathering:
Have the staff and candy canes at hand.

Gathering for Candy Canes:

After everyone has gathered round, hook the shepherd's staff gently around a member of your group. Tell them that you are pretending to be a shepherd using your staff to pull a trapped lamb from a dangerous ledge.

Next, give a biblical background about shepherds:

A shepherd is someone who takes care of a flock of sheep. Caring for sheep has never been an easy job, especially in biblical times.

Wild animals such as wolves would sometimes come and try to kill the sheep. To beat off wolves, a shepherd carried a heavy stick called a rod.

The shepherd needed to make sure the sheep were fed and given water.

He often had to move them to greener pastures and lead them to streams of water. He used a long stick with a curve at one end, called a staff, to prod them along.

Sometimes a sheep would travel away from the flock and get caught in a crevice or on a rocky ledge. A shepherd would use the crook of his staff to pull the sheep out of a dangerous situation.

A famous psalm in the Bible, written by a shepherd named David, says that God cares for us as a shepherd cares for his sheep.

Read Psalm 23:1-4.

Next, ask the group this question: What Christmas treat was created in honor of the Christmas shepherds?

The answer, of course, is candy canes!

Next offer a prayer:

Dear God,
   From now on, whenever we eat a candy cane, we will think of your loving staff surrounding us. Thank you for shepherds, thank you for candy canes, and thank you for your Son, the good Shepherd, Jesus Christ. Amen.

Pass out the candy canes.

Coins: The Widow's Mite

Nickels and quarters help us count our blessings in The Cheerful Giving Game.

Luke 21:3: "He said, 'Truly I tell you, this poor widow has put in more than all of them.' "

Preparations

Foods: chocolate coins, wrapped in foil

Materials: an ornamental box for the coins, photocopies of The Cheerful Giving Game

At Home:
   This activity promotes an awareness of our daily abundance and collects coins for a mission project.

   Locate chocolate coins, usually available at a specialty food shop, and put them in an attractive box. You will want one coin per person.

   Photocopy The Cheerful Giving Game,* one per household. This is a take-home activity:

The Cheerful Giving Game

Each day this week, put the correct amount of change in an envelope.

Sunday: 5¢ for every pair of shoes in your closet.
Monday: 5¢ for every time you talk to a friend on the phone.
Tuesday: 25¢ if you have pizza, chocolate, or ice cream.
Wednesday: 5¢ for every electrical appliance you use.
Thursday: 25¢ if you listen to music.
Friday: 5¢ for every snack you eat.
Saturday: 5¢ for every television show you watch.

Before the Gathering:
   Have copies of the game and the box of coins at hand.

Gathering to Consider Coins

When the group has gathered, open the Bible to Luke 21:1-4 and read the story of the widow's mite.

Next, hold the box and display the glittering chocolate coins. In a conversational manner, explain that this is an abundance of coins. Then distribute them.

This done, point out that one or two coins are not an abundance. Probably each recipient of a chocolate coin would prefer to keep and enjoy it. It would be harder to part with your one and only chocolate coin than to have a large box of coins and part with half of them. Compare this to the widow's offering and Jesus' observation.

Tell the group that you have a game for them to play over the course of the next week. The Cheerful Giving Game will focus on the abundance in their lives and ask recognition of this abundance through the donation of coins. Ask the group to decide to what charitable purpose they would like their coins to be given. As this is being decided, pass out photocopies of the game.

The coins can be brought to church at a convenient time in the following weeks and then given to the chosen charity.

Close with prayer:

   Father of all perfect gifts,
      Enlighten us as we hear the counsel of your servant Paul:
   "The point is this: the one who sows sparingly will also reap sparingly, and the one who sows bountifully will also reap bountifully. Each of you must give as you have made up your mind, not reluctantly or under compulsion, for God loves a cheerful giver" (II Corinthians 9:6-7).
      We give you thanks for the abundance in our lives. Strengthen our faith so that we may do good works in your name. Amen.

Invite all to save or eat their chocolate coins.

Crowns: "The Crown of Life"

Children and adults will enjoy decorating paper crowns and a crown shaped cake with jewels of candy.

James 1:12: "Blessed is anyone who endures temptation. Such a one has stood the test and will receive the crown of life that the Lord has promised to those who love him."

Preparations

Foods: Hot Milk Crown Cake (Recipe Collection) or yellow cake mix; Butter Frosting (Recipe Collection) or two 16-ounce cans prepared frosting; yellow food coloring; cake decorations such as gumdrops, M&M's, and sprinkles; beverages

Materials: heavy construction paper; elastic (elastic cord or 1/4-inch band); scissors, stapler, and glue; crayons or markers; glitter, sequins, or fabric trimmings; bowls; plates; cups; napkins; and forks

At Home:
Bake the Crown Cake.

Paper Crowns:
If you can estimate how many will attend, constructing the paper crowns at home will ensure plenty of time for decorating at the gathering.
Assemble crown by folding a standard piece of construction paper in half lengthwise. Cut crown points and staple an 8-inch piece of elastic to each end. These crowns will fit adults and children, and be sturdy enough for the children to play with for many days.

Before the Gathering:
Place the Crown Cake in the center of a table with the cake decorations in small bowls around it. A circle prayer will follow the decorating activities so allow enough space around the table for the group to gather.
On another table or tables, arrange the craft supplies.
Finally, prepare beverages and put out plates, cups, napkins, and forks.

Gathering to Decorate Crowns

Modeling a paper crown that you have decorated creates a festive atmosphere for greeting the group. When all are seated around the craft tables, ask them to guess what they will be making with the interesting materials in front of them. Of course they will answer paper crowns!
Next, introduce the Christian symbolism of crowns:

Since biblical times the crown has been a symbol of distinction. Kings, queens, priests, bridegrooms, heroes, and victorious athletes have worn crowns ranging from a wreath of greens (I Corinthians 9:25) to a circle of silver or gold studded with jewels (Zechariah 6:11; 9:16). The most noted crown to all Christians is the crown of thorns that was placed on the head of Jesus prior to his Crucifixion. Because Jesus wore this humble crown of thorns for us, Christians may one day wear the crown of eternal life.

After you have talked about the symbolism of crowns, read James 1:12.

When you have finished the passage, tell the group that the time has come to celebrate the promise of eternal life by designing fanciful paper crowns. While everyone is working on the paper crowns, invite a few at a time to take a turn at decorating the Crown Cake.

When the paper crowns are finished and the cake is decorated, ask everyone to don the crowns and gather in a circle around the cake for a prayer. Join hands with one another, extending your hands in the air to form the points of a crown. You, or someone else in the group, can say the prayer:

> Dear God, Ruler of heaven and earth,
>   Today and tomorrow, through happiness and strife, we celebrate your promise of the crown of life. Amen.

As the cake and beverages are served, encourage the group to mingle and admire the crowns.

RECIPE COLLECTION

BOWL BREAD

3 cups warm water (110°)
¾ cup honey
2 tablespoons yeast (3 packages)
1½ teaspoons salt
⅓ cup butter or margarine, melted
8 cups flour (2 to 3 cups may be whole wheat)

Pour warm water into a large mixing bowl. Add the yeast and honey. Stir to mix and set in a warm place while the yeast activates (bubbles).

While waiting, melt the butter and add the salt.

When the yeast is ready, pour the butter into the yeast mixture. Begin to work in the flour, two cups at a time, by hand or with an electric mixer. After six cups of flour have been stirred in, put the last two cups of flour on a surface for kneading. Turn out dough and knead until elastic and smooth.

Divide the dough in half and pat into 2 circles about ¾-inch thick. Shape each circle over a greased, inverted bowl that is oven-proof. Prick the surface with a fork. The bowl should be no smaller than 10 inches wide by 6 inches high.

Bake at 350° for 25-35 minutes. Cool. Loosen edges with a knife and gently remove the bread.

Yield: 2 large loaves or 50 2-by-2-inch pieces for passing around a group.

DAY AND NIGHT COOKIES

1 cup butter or margarine
1½ cups sugar
2 eggs
2¾ cups flour

2 teaspoons cream of tartar
1 teaspoon soda
¼ teaspoon salt

Cream butter or margarine, sugar, and eggs. Combine the dry ingredients and add to the first mixture. Refrigerate the dough for several hours or overnight.

Shape into balls the size of golf balls. Flatten with a glass dipped in flour.

Bake on a lightly greased cookie sheet at 375° for around 12 minutes. Remove from the pan and allow the cookies to cool before putting them into a container for storage.

Yield: 2 dozen 4-inch cookies.

BUTTER FROSTING

½ stick butter
6 cups (2 one-pound boxes) confectioner's sugar
¾ cup milk
2 teaspoons vanilla

Cream butter and beat in ½ cup sugar. Mix in ¼ cup milk and vanilla. Add the rest of the sugar and slowly mix in enough milk to make a spreadable frosting.

Yield: 4 cups.

For Crown Cake: Add yellow food coloring to create a gold crown or blue or purple for a crown lined in velvet. Frost according to the directions for Hot Milk Crown Cake.

For Day and Night Cookies: Divide the frosting into two bowls. Heat 2 ounces baking chocolate in a double boiler or microwave. Mix chocolate into one bowl of frosting. Cover frostings and refrigerate until one hour before the gathering.

RAINBOW CAKE

angel food cake batter
red, yellow, green, and blue food coloring

Prepare angel food cake batter according to a recipe or the directions for an angel food cake mix.

Divide the batter into four bowls. Add several drops of food coloring and carefully fold to create red (pink), yellow, green, and blue batters.

In a 10-inch tube-pan, gently pour a layer of pink batter, followed by layers of yellow, green, and blue (the order of the rainbow). Bake according to directions. Invert to cool. Be certain to slice slowly with a sharp, serrated knife.

Yield: 12 slices or 16 very thin slices.

STIR-UP SUNDAY CAKE

Stir-up Sunday Cake is traditionally a steamed plum pudding. This is an easier version.

½ cup butter or margarine, softened
½ cup brown sugar
½ cup sugar
6 eggs
2 teaspoons vanilla
1 cup candied fruit
1 cup raisins

1 cup nuts
2 tablespoons flour
3 cups day-old bread or buns,
    broken into large crumbs
½ teaspoon nutmeg
1 teaspoon cinnamon
½ teaspoon cloves

Cream butter or margarine and sugars. One at a time, add the eggs. Mix in vanilla. Add the spices.

Dredge the fruit, raisins, and nuts with flour. Add to the first mixture. Stir in the bread crumbs.

Grease and flour a 9-inch spring-form pan or a casserole lined with greased brown paper. Bake at 350° for 40 minutes. Use a knife to loosen the cake from the pan after it has cooled for 30 minutes.

Yield: 12 slices.

BARLEY BREAD

Barley flour is low in gluten and will not rise much. Sifting in regular or bread flour will make a larger, less heavy loaf of bread.

1½ cups milk
1½ tablespoons salt
4 tablespoons oil
½ cup warm water (110°)

½ cup honey
2 tablespoons yeast (3 packages)
2¾ cups barley flour
2¾ cups all-purpose or bread flour

Scald milk. Pour into a large mixing bowl and stir in salt and 2 tablespoons of oil. Set aside to cool to lukewarm.

In a small bowl, dissolve yeast and honey in the warm water.

While waiting for the yeast to activate (bubble), sift the two flours together and set aside.

When ready, pour the yeast mixture into the mixing bowl with the milk. Add 3 cups of flour and mix by hand or with an electric mixer. Work in one more cup of flour. Pour the rest of the flour on a surface for kneading. Knead the dough until elastic and smooth.

Divide the dough in half and shape into two loaves. With a tablespoon of oil, grease a cookie sheet. Place the loaves on the cookie sheet and brush them with the remaining oil. Cover loosely with plastic wrap or a damp cloth. Let rise for 1 hour in a warm place.

Uncover the bread and bake at 350° for 35 minutes.

Yield: 2 loaves or 24 slices.

FLOOD PUNCH

1 2-liter bottle Sprite or Seven-Up, chilled
1 46-ounce can pineapple juice, chilled
1 12-ounce can frozen concentrated pink lemonade, thawed
1 cup water
blue food coloring

In punch bowl combine Sprite or Seven-Up, pineapple juice, lemonade, and water. Add 10 or more drops of blue food coloring, until the color of the punch resembles that of sea water!

Yield: 25 5-ounce servings.

WHITE CHRISTMAS HOT CHOCOLATE

For a Small Group:

¾ cup water
6 ounces white chocolate,
    broken into pieces
¼ cup sugar
¼ teaspoon salt
4½ cups milk
1 teaspoon vanilla

Yield: 40 ounces (5 8-ounce mugs or 8 5-ounce cups)

For a Crowd:

2¼ cups water
18 ounces white chocolate,
    broken into pieces
¾ cup sugar
¾ teaspoon salt
13½ cups milk
3 teaspoons vanilla

Yield: 120 ounces or 15 8-ounce mugs/24 5-ounce cups.

In an appropriate size kettle or crockpot, heat the water to boiling. Mix in sugar, salt, and chocolate pieces. Stir constantly until the chocolate is melted. Add milk and heat. Turn off the heat and stir in vanilla.

Small candy canes make a delicious holiday garnish.

VALENTINE PIZZA

5 packages plain English muffins
1 cup plus 4 tablespoons oil (olive or vegetable)
1 jar (28 ounces) prepared spaghetti sauce
28 ounces grated mozzarella cheese
toppings for pizza such as olives, onions, peppers, mushrooms, pepperoni, hamburger, sausage, anchovies. To estimate amounts figure one tablespoon (½ ounce) per serving.

Preheat oven to 375°. With paring knife, split muffins and cut a 1-inch triangular wedge from each to create a heart shape. Set aside the wedges to use for salad croutons.

Place heart-shaped muffins on cookie sheets and brush lightly with oil. Toast for 3 to 5 minutes until muffins are hot and beginning to crisp.

Stir 4 tablespoons of oil into the spaghetti sauce. Remove muffins from oven and spoon one tablespoon of spaghetti sauce on each. Sprinkle about 2 tablespoons of grated cheese on each muffin. Return to the oven for 3 to 7 minutes until the cheese is melted.

Put the toppings in bowls and arrange salad bar style. Each person will garnish his or her own pizza.

Yield: 60 pizzas. For a luncheon or dinner count on several pizzas per person.

BIBLE GARDEN SALAD

Concoct a salad using some of the vegetables and fruits that were grown in biblical days. Serve with Scripture Salad Dressings.

lettuce	olives
onions	cucumbers
leeks	raisins
squash	dates
chick-peas	

Prepare croutons by tossing dry or toasted bread or crusts in a hot frying pan with a small amount of oil and a minced clove of garlic. If preparing Valentine Pizza, the wedges cut from the English muffins make good croutons.

SCRIPTURE SALAD DRESSINGS

Mustard Seed Dressing

1 cup plain yogurt	2 tablespoons honey
2 tablespoons lemon juice	1 tablespoon mustard seed

Mix together all ingredients. Refrigerate until serving.

Yield: 1 cup.

Parsley Vinaigrette

1 cup vinegar (wine or cider)	1 tablespoon parsley,
½ cup oil (olive or vegetable)	chopped (fresh or dried)
1 tablespoon sugar	2 cloves garlic, crushed

In a cruet, mix together the vinegar, oil, and sugar. Shake to blend. Add parsley and garlic and shake again.

Yield: 1½ cups

Both dressings will taste best if made a day ahead of serving.

WORKDAY GROUP SOUP

7 quarts water	3 tablespoons salt
3 cans (11¾ ounces) chicken or beef stock	1 tablespoon garlic
3 pounds chicken or beef	2 teaspoons black pepper
herbs	
bouillon	

At home pour water, canned broth, and meat into a covered soup kettle and cook until meat is done. Remove meat, debone, and chop. Return meat to stock and add salt, pepper, and garlic.

Along with the meat and broth, bring to the gathering a selection of herbs for seasoning the soup, such as parsley, sage, rosemary, or thyme, and bouillon cubes or granules.

At the gathering put the meat and broth into a large, canning-size kettle. Those coming to the workday will contribute canned (do not drain), frozen, or fresh vegetables. Add some herbs along with the vegetables.

Allow the soup to simmer for about an hour and a half. Add bouillon if the soup's flavor is weak and adjust seasonings to taste.

Yield: The yield for this soup varies according to the size of the group. There always seems to be at least a cup serving per person. One canning-size kettle usually holds enough soup for 80 people.

LENTIL STEW

14 cups water
4 cups lentils, rinsed
4 cups potatoes, diced
4 cups carrots, diced
4 large onions, chopped
1 can (11¾ ounces) beef stock

2 tablespoons salt
1 teaspoon pepper
1 teaspoon garlic, fresh or dried
1 teaspoon ground cumin
1 tablespoon lemon juice

Into a large kettle, pour the water and the lentils and begin to cook over medium heat. Add vegetables, beef stock, salt, and pepper. Cook over medium heat, stirring occasionally, until vegetables are tender—about one hour. Reduce heat and add garlic, cumin, and lemon juice. Simmer for 20 minutes.

Adjust seasonings to taste.

Yield: 20 1-cup servings.

FLATBREAD

3½ cups flour
½ teaspoon baking powder
1 teaspoon salt

½ cup butter or margarine, softened
1 cup milk

Combine dry ingredients. Mix in butter or margarine with a pastry blender. Add milk. Shape into 6-inch circles, ⅛-inch thick, by patting with hand.

Bake on greased cookie sheet for about 15 minutes or until golden brown.

Yield: 8 loaves.

SCRIPTURE CAKE

1 cup Judges 5:25 (butter, softened)
1 cup Jeremiah 6:20 (brown sugar)
4 Jeremiah 17:11 (eggs)
4 cups I Kings 4:22 (flour)
1 teaspoon Amos 4:5 (baking soda)
⅔ cup Proverbs 16:24 (honey)
1⅓ cups Exodus 3:8 (milk)

1½ cups Psalm 92:12 (dates)
1½ cups I Samuel 30:12 (raisins)
1 cup Numbers 17:8 (sliced almonds)
3½ teaspoons II Chronicles 9:9 (spices:
  2 teaspoons cinnamon, 1 teaspoon
  ground gloves, ½ teaspoon nutmeg)

Cream butter, sugar, and eggs. Mix in flour, baking soda, honey, and milk. Fold in dates, raisins, almonds, and spices.

Bake in a 13-by-9 greased and floured pan at 350° for around 40 minutes or until a knife inserted in the center comes out clean.

Yield: 24 2-by-2-inch servings.

ST. JOHN'S BROWNIES

½ cup butter or margarine, softened
1 cup sugar
1 cup brown sugar
2 teaspoons vanilla
3 eggs

1 cup flour
4 tablespoons carob powder
2 teaspoons baking powder
½ teaspoon salt

Cream butter or margarine and sugars. Beat in eggs and vanilla. Combine flour, carob, baking powder, and salt. Add to the first mixture.

Spread into a greased and floured 13-by-9-inch baking pan. Bake at 350° for around 25 minutes.

Yield: 24 2-inch brownies.

ICE CREAM CONE ANGELS

3 packages (36) sugar cones
32 paper lace doilies (heart shaped or round, 3 or 4 inches wide)
1 bag regular marshmallows
12-ounce tube frosting (yellow)
½ gallon ice cream
3 cans whipping cream

Place small plates, one by one, down the length of the serving table. On each plate, put a cone with the point facing up.

Assembling the Angels

For every cone, fold a paper doily in half and reopen. Using the tubed frosting, squeeze a dab on the center of the doily. Stick the doily to the cone to make the angel's wings.

With a paring knife, make a small slit in the end of a marshmallow. Gently push the marshmallow over the point of the cone. This is the angel's head.

To create a halo, squeeze frosting in a circle on the top of the marshmallow.

Do not scoop the ice cream base until serving time. Complete each angel by momentarily setting the cone off the plate, putting one scoop of ice cream on the plate, squirting a whipped cream cloud around the ice cream, and replacing the cone angel on top. Serve immediately!

Yield: 32 angels. It's best to have extra cones on hand in the event that some break during assembly.

EASY HOT CROSS BUNS

3 tablespoons sugar
1 teaspoon cinnamon
1 teaspoon cardamom
½ teaspoon nutmeg

½ cup raisins or currants
2 tablespoons butter or margarine
1 package (25 ounces) frozen roll dough
1 egg, lightly beaten

Thaw dough according to package directions.

In a small bowl, mix raisins, sugar, and spices.

Grease a mixing bowl and put in dough. Add raisin mixture. Grease hands and knead dough until all of the raisins are worked in, about 3 minutes.

Turn out dough onto a greased surface and shape into a log about 12 inches long.

Using a knife, cut the log in half lengthwise and in half across the width. Separate the 4 dough pieces.

Split each smaller log in half lengthwise, then make 3 equally spaced cuts across the width. This makes 8 dough pieces per smaller log.

Having cut 32 buns, grease hands again. Roll each bun between palms to make it smooth and round.

Place buns on greased cookie sheets and cover with damp cloths or plastic wrap. Allow to rise in a warm place for 1 hour.

Brush buns with beaten egg. Bake at 350° for 13-15 minutes or until golden brown.

Yield: 32 small buns.

BELIEVER'S FROSTING

4 tablespoons butter
¼ cup milk
3 cups confectioner's sugar

Melt butter. Stir in milk. Whisk in sugar, one cup at a time.

This frosting is to be drizzled over the buns in the sign of the cross. If frosting thickens prior to use, thin with a teaspoon of water or milk.

Yield: 1½ cups.

HOT MILK CROWN CAKE

½ cup butter
1 cup milk
5 eggs, separated
2 cups sugar

2 teaspoons vanilla
2 rounded teaspoons baking powder
2 cups flour

Heat butter and milk until the butter melts. Do not allow the milk to boil.
Whip egg whites until stiff. Set aside.
Beat egg yolks, then add sugar and vanilla. Combine baking powder and flour and mix into the egg yolks. Stir in the egg whites.
Add the hot milk and melted butter. Mix quickly.
Bake at 350° in a greased and floured 13-by-9-inch pan until done, around 35 minutes.
While the cake is baking, cover a cookie sheet with aluminum foil or paper doilies.
When cooled, loosen the edges of the cake. Cut the cake in the shape of a crown as shown in the diagram below:

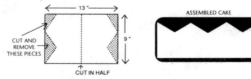

With a knife remove the shaded triangles. Enjoy for a snack.
Cut the crown cake in half and carefully lift the halves with a spatula. Place the crown back together on the cookie sheet.
Frost with tinted butter frosting. Cover for transporting to the gathering.

Yield: about 24 1-by-3-inch slices.

If a large crowd is expected, connect two crown cakes and serve on a large tray or board covered in foil or bake and frost two or more separate cakes.